Cambridge Ele

CW00551727

Elements in Ancient Egypt
edited by
Gianluca Miniaci
University of Pisa
Juan Carlos Moreno García
CNRS, Paris
Anna Stevens
University of Cambridge and Monash University

THE ARCHAEOLOGY OF EGYPTIAN NON-ROYAL BURIAL CUSTOMS IN NEW KINGDOM EGYPT AND ITS EMPIRE

Wolfram Grajetzki
University College London

CAMBRIDGE
UNIVERSITY PRESS

CAMBRIDGE
UNIVERSITY PRESS

University Printing House, Cambridge CB2 8BS, United Kingdom

One Liberty Plaza, 20th Floor, New York, NY 10006, USA

477 Williamstown Road, Port Melbourne, VIC 3207, Australia

314–321, 3rd Floor, Plot 3, Splendor Forum, Jasola District Centre,
New Delhi – 110025, India

103 Penang Road, #05–06/07, Visioncrest Commercial, Singapore 238467

Cambridge University Press is part of the University of Cambridge.

It furthers the University's mission by disseminating knowledge in the pursuit of
education, learning, and research at the highest international levels of excellence.

www.cambridge.org
Information on this title: www.cambridge.org/9781009073509
DOI: 10.1017/9781009064521

First published 2021

A catalogue record for this publication is available from the British Library.

ISBN 978-1-009-07350-9 Paperback
ISSN 2516-4813 (online)
ISSN 2516-4805 (print)

The Archaeology of Egyptian Non-Royal Burial Customs in New Kingdom Egypt and Its Empire

Elements in Ancient Egypt in Context

DOI: 10.1017/9781009064521
First published online: December 2021

Wolfram Grajetzki
University College London
Author for correspondence: Wolfram Grajetzki, WlfrmG@aol.com

Abstract: This Element provides a new evaluation of burial customs in New Kingdom Egypt, from about 1550 to 1077 BC, with an emphasis on burials of the wider population. It also covers the regions then under Egyptian control: the Southern Levant and the area of Nubia as far as the Fourth Cataract. The inclusion of foreign countries provides insights not only into the interaction between the centre of the empire and its conquered regions, but also concerning what is typically Egyptian and to what extent the conquered regions were culturally influenced. It can be shown that burials in Lower Nubia closely follow those in Egypt. In the Southern Levant, by contrast, cemeteries of the period often yield numerous Egyptian objects, but burial customs in general do not follow those in Egypt.

Keywords: burial, Egypt, class, Nubia, Levant

ISBNs: 9781009073509 (PB), 9781009064521 (OC)
ISSNs: 2516-4813 (online), 2516-4805 (print)

Contents

1   Introduction   1

2   Burial Traditions in Ancient Egypt   6

3   Space: Tombs and Graves   20

4   Burial Goods: Daily Life versus Objects of Funerary Industry   27

5   Summaries   49

6   Concluding Remarks   61

   Abbreviations   63

   Appendix: Examples of Burials and Cemeteries   64

   Glossary   73

   References   75

1 Introduction

This Element aims to provide an evaluation of Egyptian burial customs in the New Kingdom, the time from about 1539 to 1077 BC. It will cover not only Egypt proper but also those regions under Egyptian control. These include the Southern Levant and Egyptian-ruled Nubia (Fig. 1). The inclusion of foreign countries provides insight into the interaction between the centre of the empire and its conquered regions, but it might also offer insights about what is typical Egyptian and to what extent the conquered regions were culturally influenced.

This Element is a by-product of a project re-evaluating the cemeteries of Rifeh, in Upper Egypt. While assessing the archaeological remains of that site, it very quickly became clear that the New Kingdom remains there are as important as those belonging to the Middle Kingdom. Middle Kingdom Rifeh is famous for its soul houses but also for the Tomb of Two Brothers. The New Kingdom finds are less spectacular, but precisely for this reason they provide an ideal view of a New Kingdom provincial cemetery, despite all the shortcomings of early 20th-century recording and publication.

One further reason for writing this Element is to counterbalance the permanent top-down view of society within Egyptology. Although there are many re-evaluations that challenge this approach to society, it certainly persists. Already the expression 'top-down view' is dubious. Most readers will understand the meaning, but putting one social group, and indeed the smallest one in a society, at the 'top' is problematic. In the same way, dividing society into elites and non-elites – as all too often has been done in recent years – is troublesome. The bulk of the population is defined by not belonging to the smallest segment of society. It is possible to compare this to the highly offensive term 'non-white', where white people are seen as 'normal' and all the others are not (Bosmajian 1969, 264). For an archaeological approach to burials, the terms 'richly equipped tomb' and 'poorly equipped burial' seem to be more suitable. They just imply that more resources were invested into one burial than into another one without any indication of the social status of the dead person.

In summaries on burial customs, most often objects especially made for the burial stand at the heart of the discussion. These include coffins, canopic jars (vessels for the separately embalmed entrails), shabtis (a helper in the afterlife) and amulets. The decoration of tomb chapels is another focal point. Egyptian tombs of the wealthiest people often have a decorated tomb chapel, which was open to those bringing offerings for the deceased. However, as it will be shown, these features are not typical for burials of most people, and not even typical for wealthier people in the provinces.

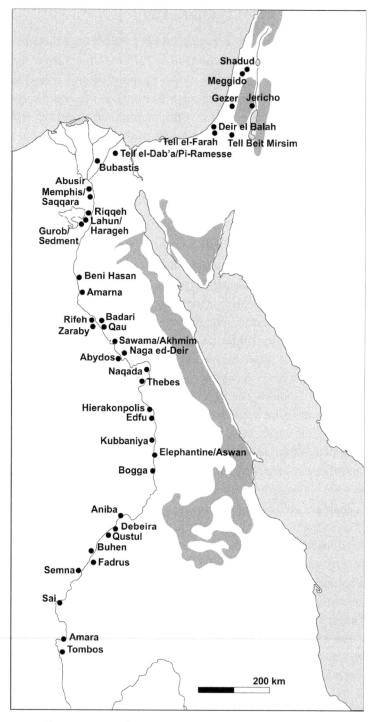

Figure 1 Map of Egypt, Nubia and the Southern Levant
in the New Kingdom (drawing: author)

In the early 18th Dynasty, around 1539 BC, Egypt was united after a period when foreigners coming from the Levant, known in later traditions as the Hyksos, had conquered parts of the Delta. Egypt itself, after their expulsion, now conquered parts of Nubia, and also parts of the Levant came under its control. Lower Nubia had already been in the Middle Kingdom under Egyptian rule. In the Second Intermediate Period, the region became part of the powerful Nubian empire of Kerma, but it seems that Egyptians still lived in the region. The material culture of the area became Egyptian. The New Kingdom rule of the Egyptians in Nubia came close to being colonisation (Smith 2003, 83–96; Smith 2015). Local families were incorporated into the Egyptian administration. They took over Egyptian titles and writing. The material culture in Lower Nubia, the region closest to Egypt, remained very much Egyptian.

In contrast, in the Levant several city states flourished with their own culture that did not change much with the arrival of and takeover by the Egyptians. It seems that the Levantine provinces were rather loose vassal states that had to pay tributes and offer military aid when needed, but often acted quite independently. Egyptian objects appear often in burials and even Egyptian-style coffins were produced. However, the underlying burial customs and beliefs were most likely still Levantine (Braunstein 2011).

Over the periods of Egyptian history and across different social classes, Egyptian burials contained different types of objects, evidently with various functions in rituals or for the afterlife. Some objects seem to come from rituals performed at or before the burial. They are often not easy to identify. A prime example is the pottery. It might be used in rituals, but vessels might also have been intended as food containers for the nourishment of the deceased. Next to items used in rituals, there are also objects especially made for the tomb. The most important one is evidently the coffin. Many amulets were perhaps also made especially for burials, but here again some amulet types might have been previously worn in daily life. The borders between daily life and funeral objects appear fluid (Pinch 2003). Daily life objects are common in burials too, especially in those of people with few resources. Pottery vessels and personal adornments are frequently used at all social levels.

Knowledge about the archaeology of grave goods is essential for understanding Egyptian material culture. Objects found in burials are on average much better preserved than those found in settlement sites. A bead necklace excavated in an undisturbed burial, well recorded, could tell us how beads were arranged on a necklace. With a few exceptions, such as in Amarna (Frankfort, Pendlebury 1933, 18), beads found at a settlement site will be loose without their stringing (Frankfort, Pendlebury 1933, 44).

While there is a popular conception that burials were stuffed with daily life objects, this is only true for the Early Dynastic Period (around 3000 to 2800 BC) and the 18th Dynasty (1539–1292 BC). However, even in these periods, particular types of objects were selected and not everything that belonged to a person's household was placed into a burial. Poorer people might make a selection due to limited resources, but even in the wealthiest tombs not everything was there. One example would be tools which are rarely a part of burial equipment in most periods of Egypt's history but also do not appear often in those periods when daily life objects are common in burials.

In most other periods (Table 1), the range of material going into an Egyptian burial was more restricted than in the Early Dynastic Period or the 18th Dynasty. This selection of objects limits heavily our knowledge of daily life objects for certain periods. One striking illustration of this is leather. It has been argued that leather working was not well developed in the Old Kingdom as there are so few finds of leather from this period (van Driel-Murray 2000, 308). However, artefacts made of leather do not belong to the types of objects chosen to go into the burial chamber in this period. The missing leather works of the Old Kingdom just reflect a gap in the archaeological record based on the specific burial customs of the day.

Table 1 Chronology
All dates BC if not otherwise stated. Egyptian dates follow Hornung, Krauss, Warburton 2006, dates before the New Kingdom are rounded up.

Egypt	Southern Levant	Nubia
Badarian Period about 4000		
Naqada Period 4000–2900		A-Group
Early Dynastic Period 1st to 3rd Dynasty 2900–2550	Late Early Bronze Age I to II	A-Group
Old Kingdom 4th to 6th Dynasty 2550–2150	Early Bronze Age III	unknown
First Intermediate Period 8th to 11th Dynasty 2150–2000	Intermediate Bronze Age	C-Group
Middle Kingdom 11th to 13th Dynasty 2000–1650	Intermediate Bronze Age to Middle Bronze Age II	C-Group
Second Intermediate Period 14th to 17th Dynasty 1650–1539	Middle Bronze Age III	C-Group, Kerma Empire

Table 1 (cont.)

Egypt	Southern Levant	Nubia
New Kingdom **18th Dynasty** Ahmose (II) 1539–1514 Amenhotep I 1514–1494 Thutmose I 1493–1483	Late Bronze Age IA	Egyptian occupation
Thutmose II 1482–1480 Hatshepsut 1479–1458 Thutmose III 1470–1425	Late Bronze Age IB	
Amenhotep II 1425–1400 Thutmose IV 1400–1390 Amenhotep III 1390–1353	Late Bronze Age IB	

Amarna Period
   Akhenaten 1353–1336
   Smenkhkare/Neferuaten
   1336–1334
   Tutankhamun 1334–1324
   Aya 1323–1320
 Haremhab 1319–1292
	Late Bronze Age IIA	

Ramesside Period **(19th and 20th Dynasty)** 19th Dynasty Ramses I 1292–1291 Sety I 1290–1279 Ramses II 1279–1213 Merenptah 1213–1203	Late Bronze Age IIB	
Sety II 1202–1200 Siptah 1197–1193 Tawesret 1192–1191	Late Bronze Age III, Iron Age I A	

20th Dynasty
 Sethnakht 1190–1188
 Ramses III 1187–1157
 Ramses IV to Ramses XI
   1156–1077
	Late Bronze Age III,
	   Iron Age I B	

Third Intermediate Period Dynasty 21 to 25 1076–655	Iron Age IIA to IIB	
Late Period Dynasty 26 664–525	Iron Age III	Kingdom of Napata
Persian Period Dynasty 27 525–404	Persian Period	

Table 1 (cont.)

Egypt	Southern Levant	Nubia
Late Dynastic Period Dynasty 28 to 30 404–343	Persian Period	
Second Persian Period 343–332	Persian Period	
Ptolemaic Period 332–30	Hellenistic Period	Kingdom of Meroe
Roman Period 30 BC–AD 395	Roman Period	

2 Burial Traditions in Ancient Egypt

2.1 Belief in an Afterlife

From religious texts as well as from the elaborate burial equipment, it is clear that Egyptians had a belief in an afterlife. The information about this often appears rather confusing to us, not adding up to a unified picture as we would like to receive it. Texts, including religious spells, were found in many burials of wealthy people of the Middle and New Kingdom. In the Middle Kingdom they appear most often on coffins, in the New Kingdom often (but not exclusively) on papyri. Today the latter are called the Book of the Dead. The ancient Egyptian name of the collection of spells was Going out at Daylight. According to this religious literature, the passage to the Underworld was complicated and at several points dangerous, as there were demons blocking the journey. One important station on the way was the judgement of Osiris, who was the god of the Underworld. In meeting this god, the deceased faced judgement of the good and bad deeds in their life. The heart of the deceased was placed on a scale against a weight representing Truth (in Egyptian *Maat*). If the bad deeds of the deceased weighed more than the good ones, they faced a composite crocodile-lion-hippopotamus monster called Ammit, 'the Devourer', that would eat them and they would face eternal death. Those who passed could enter eternal life in the Underworld (Assmann 2001, 73–7).

In the Underworld, located in the west where the sun sets, life seems to have been similar to that on earth; tomb scenes commonly show the deceased ploughing fields or at the harvest. There was, evidently, the permanent fear that the deceased might not have enough to eat. Many spells in the Book of the Dead tackle this problem (Assmann 2001, 128–30).

New Kingdom written sources refer to different aspects of individuals, including words we translate as 'body' and 'shadow', but also words we translate as 'soul'. However, soul might not be an adequate translation for them. These 'souls' are aspects of the human being that became especially important in the afterlife. The concepts are often hard to understand, as there is nothing directly comparable in current major religions. One of them is called Ba. As a Ba, the deceased transformed, as attested from the New Kingdom on, into a bird with a human head and was able to move around freely (Assmann 2001, 90–1). The Ka was perhaps the most important aspect (Assmann 2001, 44). It represents the power of life. Its symbol is a pair of raised arms, but Kas are normally depicted as human, as a double of the deceased person. The food offerings for the deceased went to their Ka. The offering formula, a short text found on many inscribed objects, especially in funerary contexts, always wishes the offerings should go to the Ka of the deceased. The Akh (Janák 2013) is the third Egyptian concept of soul and the most difficult one to understand. *Akh* is an Egyptian word for 'light' or 'illumination' and the Akh is most often shown as a crested ibis, but it is doubtful whether the Egyptians really saw the Akh as a bird. The deceased only became an Akh after death, and becoming an Akh was one important transformation. As an Akh the deceased became powerful and was able to protect tombs (Otto 1975). *Akh* could also mean 'useful' and on becoming an Akh, the deceased could be useful for the living (Assmann 2001, 339).

In the coffin, the deceased was identified with the Underworld god Osiris. The coffin was identified as the sky goddess Nut, who was the mother of Osiris. Placing the deceased in the coffin placed them into the womb of their mother (Assmann 2001, 170–3).

It remains difficult to see how much these concepts of the Underworld were understood by everybody. It might be assumed that most people of all social levels had some ideas of these aspects of human beings, but the refined versions were perhaps known only by some specialists, in this case, funerary priests.

There is some debate in Egyptology over whether the body of the deceased needed to be preserved for eternity. The development of mummification seems to be a strong indicator for this. In general, special care for the body is visible in burials. This contrasts with the record from the Southern Levant. However, most Egyptians were not properly mummified, and their bodies soon decayed. Egyptians must have been aware of this, but they still equipped their burials with all types of goods, at least in certain periods. They evidently believed in an afterlife, even if they knew that their bodies would not survive apart from some bones (Willems 2014, 140–1).

2.2 Burials of the Working Population

Burials of 'poorer' people had been described early on by Gaston Maspero (1895, 167–9) in a general book on Ancient Egypt, even though his main focus was the graves and the tombs of the most wealthy people. More than half a century later, Walter Bryan Emery included in his general account, *Archaic Egypt*, a separate section on burial customs within the chapter on religion (Emery 1961, 128–64). The burial customs chapter is more an architectural guide to Early Dynastic tombs rather than a description of burial customs as, for example, burial goods are hardly mentioned. However, this chapter also includes quite detailed descriptions of burials for people that he regards as belonging outside the ruling class: the peasantry (Emery 1961: 139).

Nevertheless, in Egyptology there is the discussion whether archaeologists have excavated burials of the working population, those of the farmers and craftsmen of Ancient Egypt, or whether the burials so far excavated do not include these people. There are opposing views on this subject within Egyptology. One extreme opinion proposes that many Egyptians did not have any formal burial at all and bodies of those who could not afford it were just thrown away with little or no formal procedure or any religious rituals (Baines, Lacovara 2002, 12–14). It has also been argued that bodies of people from the poorer segments of society were just thrown into the water (Niwiński 2014).

Clearly it is very hard, or even impossible, to identify the social level of people in graves. As already indicated, there seems to be a certain tendency in Egyptology to assume that not many burials of the working population were preserved (Weill 1938; Baines, Lacovara 2002, 12–14; Driaux 2019, 8–9). This hypothesis might in some cases reflect a lack of knowledge about the archaeological record in general, but it might also relate to certain assumptions automatically made about burials of the working population. In this particular case, there seems to be the hypothesis that farmers and craftsmen, the bulk of the Egyptian population, did not own anything. The majority of the population is identified as the poor part of society and is almost automatically equated with destitution. In this view, only those burials with few or no burial goods can belong to the working population.

Baines and Lacovara (2002, 13) took the cemeteries on Elephantine as their main example for arguing that a high percentage of burials, and especially of the working population, are missing. According to them the poorest segment of society is not visible in the records. About 10 per cent of Elephantine's burial grounds was excavated, with about 248 burials for 500 years, yielding an extremely low population number of about 2,500 deaths in this period; this would indicate about 125 people living on Elephantine at any given time, taking

25 years as average age of death. Some more burials can be expected at Qubbet el Hawa, opposite the island, where the richer segments of the society were placed. Although the settlement on Elephantine was doubtless very small in the Old Kingdom, about 125 people seems too low. However, several other factors have to be taken into account. One of them is the reuse of tombs and burial places in general. Many burials dating to the earlier part of this 500-year occupation period on Elephantine might have been destroyed by later activities. Especially in more densely packed cemeteries in Egypt, the reuse of older burial shafts and chambers is often detectable. An extreme example is the Theban necropolis with the permanent reuse of tombs (see for example Graefe 2007). Furthermore, only 10 per cent of the cemeteries on Elephantine were excavated and there is not much we can say about the other parts of the burial ground. There might be parts packed with simple surface burials that would fit more closely the expectations of some researchers about 'poor' burials. In addition, Elephantine is a small island and many more burial grounds might be expected on the lands on the west and east of the island. Indeed, further Old Kingdom burial grounds were recently identified at Aswan, east of the island (von Pilgrim 2021, 399). Taking just one burial ground to calculate the number of burials in one funerary landscape of a rather small settlement seems problematic.

There are further, rather negative, views on the burials of the broader population. One example is Baines (2009, 118–21) discussing the Old Kingdom cemetery at Naga ed-Deir, excavated by George A. Reisner at the beginning of the 20th century. Reisner argued that the cemetery belonged to a small, rural community. Baines argued against that and wondered whether Naga ed-Deir was in fact the cemetery for Thinis, the provincial capital town. He points to the high status objects found in some tombs and the elaborate architecture of some of them. Furthermore, he observed that few tombs were looted and that almost no burials overlap others, showing that there was a respect for older burials that indicates a 'well integrated and consistent' community. According to Baines, this cannot be the burial place of ordinary farmers. That conclusion would imply that ordinary farmers did not respect the dead, and did not form well-integrated and consistent communities.

These views are contested by other scholars. Under Barry Kemp, several cemeteries have been excavated at King Akhenaten's capital city Amarna, and for him and his team, there is no doubt that they belonged to 'commoners' (Kemp 2013, 256). Stephan Seidlmayer argues for the cemeteries in the Qau-Badari, Matmar, Mostaggeda region (in Upper Egypt, just east and south of Asyut) that the graves found were mainly the burial places of the farming population in nearby villages. He refers to the simple tomb form and simple burial equipment (Seidlmayer 1990, 206–7).

In addition, there seems to be in Egyptology a certain tendency to conflate the terms poor and farmers. Evidently, a definition of poor people is needed (Driaux 2019). What does 'poor' mean? Are all Egyptian farmers automatically poor people? Is there in the burials a difference between carpenters, fishermen or herdsmen? Can we assume that these people are all automatically poor or are there also differences between some farmers and other farmers? Were carpenters better off? Are there distinctions of wealth between those farmers living on 'poor' land and those who are lucky with fertile land providing them with a rich harvest each year? Or was the rich harvest taken away by local 'tax' collectors? We have little knowledge about land ownership in Ancient Egypt (Janssen 1975, 141–2). Did most farmers own their land or did they work on estates of officials or on estates of institutions such as temples? Here, I prefer to label these people the working population rather than the poor. Clearly, some people might have been really poor, always at the edge of survival, but others might have had a fairly stable income, more than just enough to survive. However, in the archaeological record it is most often only possible to speculate.

This Element presents a high percentage of burials of the New Kingdom that most likely do not belong to the wealthiest section of society. It will be assumed that a substantial proportion of those burials found in provincial cemeteries belong to the working population of these regions. Certainly, there were also some wealthier people in the provinces. Towns had local governors, and probably other officials on the local level, people who were doubtless better off. Most of the burials that were found in the provinces do not have a tomb stone that could tell us the name and profession of the deceased. Inscribed coffins that would provide similar information are extremely rare. The social level of a very high number of buried people remains enigmatic and open to speculation. A social reading of burials remains a complicated task (Lemos 2017, 123–4).

It is evident that the resources of the working population were limited. It can be expected that they did not have much in the way of assets for acquiring elaborate objects. As these people plausibly also had some expectations for an afterlife, they would presumably have made some arrangements. After all, it can be supposed that they might have had some commodities at home. Even the very poorest of the working population must have had some pottery vessels for storing, preparing and eating food. They would also have had clothes. Furniture might have been quite expensive and we might not expect it in the houses of the poorest, but they would propably have had mats for sleeping on and baskets for storing some items. At Tell el-Dab'a in the Eastern Delta, an early Middle Kingdom settlement with miniscule houses was excavated, offering a view on the living conditions of the working population. The finds there include pottery, stone tools, but also beads and scarabs. The latter provide evidence for personal adornment (Czerny 1999). A similar picture emerges when looking at the smaller houses at Amarna. The south-western corner of the northern suburb consists mainly of smaller and a few middle-sized buildings (Frankfort, Pendlebury 1933, plate IX). These houses were found full of small finds: there was pottery, but also many items of personal adornment, such as pendants, beads and rings, and even a bronze knife and limestone figures of monkeys (Frankfort, Pendlebury 1933, 51, 84–90). Especially the social level of those people living at Amarna is far from certain and it might be argued that these are the living places of some better off servants working for the wealthier people in the bigger houses that are not far away. However, these houses certainly do not belong to the wealthiest people, and yet those living here had some belongings.

These two examples provide evidence that poorer people had some access to a certain range of objects. At first sight, this result seems rather banal. But these findings have to be compared with burials, as all too often even burials with just a few objects are seen as belonging to some richer parts of society (Baines 2006, 17). In this context, the findings from the settlements have clear significance. There is no reason to assert that burials with a small or even bigger selection of objects could not belong to people of the working population.

There are further arguments to note concerning the burials of the working population. Janet Richards (2005, 66) observed that it is easy to dig and arrange a surface burial and it is hard to imagine that not everybody was aiming for it. However, on top of that, there is no reason to assume that even poorer segments of society might not undertake something more complex. Bricking up a small underground chamber is most likely manageable within one day or two days. Imagine that a man or woman in a farming community died around forty years old, with five sons or daughters in their early twenties. It must have been fairly easy for them to arrange something more complex within a few days.

It is also instructive to compare simple burials uncovered all around Egypt, with similar burials found in other cultures. There are many prehistoric societies with elaborate burial customs. Many of these societies did not have any advanced social stratification. The simplicity of the funerary architecture is often the same. Burial equipment is also often comparable. There are a few pots, there are personal adornments and sometimes tools and weapons. In many cultures, women were buried with personal adornments, men sometimes with weapons. It seems odd to argue that in the case of Ancient Egypt, these burials belong to better-off people, while it is agreed that those people in pre-state societies are simple farmers. One example for comparison could be C-group graves in Lower Nubia (Hafsaas 2021). These are often simple surface burials, but many of them have stone tumuli. Burial goods include pottery and personal adornments. The expenditure for these graves cannot be much different to many of the less elaborate burials found all through Egypt and seems to be often more time consuming. Now, the C-group people (about 2500 to 1500 BC) are most often regarded as herdsmen (Hafsaas 2021, 159–60). Yet, according to some Egyptologists, comparable burials in Egypt belong already to a slightly wealthier segment of society. There are certainly different factors involved, making such a comparison complicated. The C-group people also had a ruling class (Hafsaas 2021, 159–64). So it might be argued that those C-group burials belong to the better off members of the C-group people. C-group cemeteries are also attested in southern Egypt. A larger one was excavated at Kubbaniya, another one near Hierakonpolis. The tomb architecture of these graves is substantial, with some having above-ground mud-brick structures forming circles. The field director at Hierakonpolis discusses whether these are soldiers or whether these people had been living here for longer and co-existed with the Egyptians (Friedman 2007).

2.3 A Long Tradition: Burials before the New Kingdom, General Remarks

Regarding burial goods, there are visible two funerary traditions in Ancient Egypt. Especially the working population and people in the provinces most often placed objects already used in daily life into the burials. These are pottery vessels, and items that had been close to the body. Generally, these include personal adornments, cosmetic objects, but also sometimes weapons or a headrest (best described for the Old Kingdom: Seidlmayer 2001). In contrast, burials of wealthy people often had objects especially made for the tomb. These are decorated coffins, statues, but could also include funerary version of personal adornments or model vessels. In the Middle Kingdom, the second funerary tradition dominated the burials of wealthy people. In the early New Kingdom, daily life objects are even common in burials of wealthy people, while objects made for the tomb are rare (apart from the coffin). In the second half of the New Kingdom, daily life objects disappeared. Burials now only contain items made for the burial.

Against general expectations, it seems that it was not always regarded as important to fill burials with objects. There are many periods in Egyptian history when even tombs of the wealthiest people are without many burial goods or even empty. One of these periods is the classical pyramid age, the Egyptian Old Kingdom, around 2600 to 2400 BC. Burials, even for officials close to the king, were most often equipped with only a very limited set of objects or even without any (Grajetzki 2003, 21–6; Smith 2017, 52). A good example of the latter option is a mastaba of the 4th Dynasty excavated at Thebes (Arnold 1976, 15; compare Roth 1988). The person buried here must have had substantial resources. He was placed under a monumental mud-brick structure, but had decided to put his resources into building the mastaba and not into burial goods. His burial chamber was found intact but did not contain any burial goods at all. His body was just found on the ground of the chamber. Perhaps there were once some wooden objects and the body might have been wrapped in linen, but this is all gone. The empty tomb chamber led even the excavator to assume that it was looted by the workmen arranging the burial. Here a lack of awareness of burial customs went together with a heavily negative view of the working population. Another example is the so-called burial of Khnumhotep at Rifeh dating to the second half of the 12th Dynasty, around 1800 BC. This burial contained four sets of coffins, two pottery vessels and a few simple personal adornments. The coffins are well made and inscribed and even partly covered with silver foil (Grajetzki 2014a). Again, the four people here had substantial resources, which went into the coffins and not into many further burial goods.

As already indicated, burial goods are not common in the Old Kingdom, but at that period there appear for the first time objects especially made for the tomb (in addition to coffins). These were miniature metal tools (Odler 2014), miniature vessels and of course the coffin and canopic jars. However, it should be clearly emphasised that most burials of this period did not have any funeral goods. Therefore, in the cemeteries, the working population disappears almost totally from the archaeological record. This is the age when the pyramids were built and when many high officials were buried under huge stone-built mastabas. These are places for the cult of the dead; all efforts went into the cult of the deceased, while the underground parts of burials were less important (Grajetzki 2003, 15–21).

Burial goods became more common at the end of the Old Kingdom, around 2300 BC. In this period, tombs of wealthier people contained a number of objects especially made for the burial, including the first mummy masks, coffins were more often inscribed and there are burials with wooden models showing small figures of farmers, craftsmen and other servants at work or bringing offerings. In the Middle Kingdom, from about 2000 to 1850 BC, coffins are often well decorated with funerary texts and images of objects used in funerary rituals. The texts are known in Egyptology as Coffin Texts. Such burials are common till the mid-12th Dynasty around 1850 BC (Garstang 1907). The focus of a wealthy burial can be summarised as the body of the deceased, well wrapped in linen and equipped with a mummy mask and lain in an inscribed coffin. Wooden models showing servants and craftsmen were arranged around the coffin or placed into a special chamber. Pottery vessels appear too. The main aim is therefore to secure the eternal food supply through pottery vessels and the wooden models. The deceased is arranged like a god-like being. Texts provide her or him with guidance in the afterlife.

After that, in the late Middle Kingdom and Second Intermediate Period (about 1850 to 1539 BC), a reduction of burial goods is again visible. The wooden models disappeared and coffins became rather simple. Only a few coffins were decorated with Coffin Texts. At Thebes, mummiform-shaped coffins became the most common type, at least for the most wealthy people. At other places, away from Thebes, mummiform coffins were not common at all, but wealthier people had mummy masks. It seems that many aspects important in the Middle Kingdom disappeared, but the body of the deceased remained central.

In contrast to these burials of the wealthiest people, graves of farmers, craftsmen and other workers were evidently much simpler. They did not contain many objects of a funerary industry but instead a range of things once used in daily life, taken from the house and the belongings of the dead and perhaps provided by family members or even friends. Overall, items that had been close to the body are the most common. These are often personal adornments, for men and more often for women. Men are sometimes equipped with weapons, but this is not a regular custom. Women also often had cosmetic boxes placed in the burial close to their bodies, containing further personal adornments but also containers for ointments and perfumes, as well as combs and hairpins. Such object types appear from the Badarian Period (about 4400 to 4000 BC) onwards up to the end of the 18th Dynasty and beyond. These object types form a kind of base for burials of people with a few resources. Pottery vessels too are common in burials of the working population (Seidlmayer 2001).

From the Naqada Period onwards, women's burials are quite often more richly equipped than those of men due to the placing of personal adornments and cosmetic items into the graves. This is not necessarily a sign of higher status of women (compare the remark for the Nubian A-Group, Gatto 2021, 133). Here a sentence from the novel *Moderato Cantabile* by Marguerite Duras might be quoted: 'The evening will be a success. The women have never been more radiant. The men covered them with jewels in proportion to their fortunes' – *Les hommes les couvrirent de bijoux au prorata de leurs bilans* (Moskos 1984, 40, n. 51).

Cemeteries of the working population are evidently harder to find in the archaeological record in periods when, in general, fewer objects were placed into burials. This is evident for almost the whole first millennium BC (Quack 2009). For that entire period burials for less well-off people are almost invisible. They did not contain any objects and were therefore not often the target of excavations. By contrast, burials of wealthy people contained almost exclusively objects especially made for burials. These include most importantly coffins, often richly decorated with painted scenes of the Underworld and the deceased offering to Underworld deities. In some of these wealthier burials appear the 'Books of the Dead' and there are often also shabtis. It seems that people without the resources to buy those elaborate, sometimes well-crafted items, did not opt to put daily life objects into burials, in stark contrast to other periods. This was evidently no longer seen as important for the passage into the afterlife. Although burials for poorer people become almost invisible in the archaeological record, there are several examples that these burials indeed existed. Here, just two cases should be mentioned. At Matmar, a cemetery of the Third Intermediate Period was excavated. Many burials there most likely belong to those not so wealthy people. Coffins were not preserved at this site due to bad organic preservation condition. The only surviving burial goods were some scarabs, a few personal adornments and amulets. Pottery vessels are rare (Brunton 1948, 73–90, pls. LIV–LVI). At Abusir was found a mass burial where many bodies were placed in a corner of an old building without any visible order. The few burial goods are personal adornments and amulets dating the burials to the Third Intermediate Period (Schäfer 1908, 113–14). Both examples, Matmar and Abusir are not very attractive for any excavators focused on objects. Especially in older excavation reports they might be just ignored and not seen as important enough to be mentioned.

The periods where it was common to place many objects into a burial are evidently also those where there is good evidence for burials of the working population. These are mainly the Naqada and early Dynastic Period (4000 to 2700 BC), the late Old Kingdom to the Early Middle Kingdom (2300 to 2000 BC) and again the late Second Intermediate Period to the early 18th Dynasty (1600 to 1450 BC).

2.4 Examples of Burial Grounds for Poorer People

The following chronological list provides examples of excavated burial grounds that most likely belong to villages or at least to people that are not members of the ruling class. The list is in no way exhaustive but should provide an idea that those cemeteries are not few. The selected sites date from the late Old Kingdom up to the late Middle Kingdom followed by the New Kingdom.

Burial grounds of poorer people and single poorer burials were found at excavations at almost all major sites. Simple burials were rarely the main target of expeditions and were recorded more as a 'side effect' at excavations on more monumental buildings or tombs. As the bigger monuments were the main aim, the lesser tombs are often just mentioned, rather than described in detail (compare Arnold 2002, pls. 8, 40, 123, 130). Special finds are sometimes noted, but rarely is a full grave presented with all objects found.

Zaraby: the cemetery near the modern village of Zaraby, is some kilometres south of Rifeh and dates to the end of the Old Kingdom. About 126 burials were found. Most are simple surface graves. Burial goods include pottery vessels, most often just one, in only one instance six vessels were found; there are cosmetic boxes, and about eight mirrors appear, as well as beads and button seals. Seven times it is attested that the body was placed within a rectangular wooden coffin (Petrie 1907, 10; Grajetzki 2020a, 128).

Harageh, cemetery D: the burial ground dates perhaps to the end of the First Intermediate Period or early Middle Kingdom. Near the modern village of Harageh, at the entrance to the Fayum were excavated about 600 tombs dating from Naqada Period, about 3500 BC to the New Kingdom and beyond. What is called in archaeology the cemetery of Harageh is in reality a number of smaller and larger burial grounds on a desert hill surrounded by fields. Cemetery D lies on the south side of this hill, while most other cemeteries are on the north side. Twenty-two burials were found, most of them simple surface burials dated around 2000 BC. Burial goods include pottery vessels, beads and amulets, including button seals. The number of burial goods in single graves is never very high. Only two burials stand out. These are two decorated burial chambers, one belonging to a man called Heryshefnakht, the other one to a woman called Wadjethotep. One wonders whether this was the burial place of a small estate. According to this idea, the two decorated burial chambers belong to the estate owner and his wife, while the much less elaborate burials would belong to the people working on the estate (Engelbach 1923, 2, pl. LVII, compare Seidlmayer 1990, 234–46).

Gurob, First Intermediate Period: this is a site close to the Fayum with a substantial cemetery belonging to the New Kingdom. Beside this, about ninety-six burials belong to two First Intermediate Period burial grounds. The graves are small and mainly surface burials. The earlier burials are often without coffins, while later coffins became more common. Pottery vessels are the most common burial item, but there are thirty-eight burials without even one pot. In a few burials personal adornments are attested (Brunton, Engelbach 1927, 6–8, pls. IX–X, compare Seidlmayer 1990, 341–7).

Harageh, Wady I and Wady II: two burial grounds dating to the late Middle Kingdom, sometimes cited, although belonging to the least well published (Baines, Lacovara 2002, 13; Driaux 2019, 9). They are briefly described, as burials of the poorer classes. Burials were packed so close to each other that the excavator had difficulties to separate tombs and objects. Nevertheless, pottery and beads are mentioned, so at least some graves had burial goods (Engelbach 1923, 2–3).

Harageh, New Kingdom: in the late Middle Kingdom, Harageh may have been one of several burial grounds for the population at Lahun, the town near the pyramid of Senusret II. The Lahun region lost importance within the Second Intermediate Period and was no longer an urban or administrative centre. In the New Kingdom, the burial ground at Harageh was still used and might have served some local farming communities. About sixty-five graves date to the New Kingdom, mostly to the 18th Dynasty. These are most often surface burials, but Middle Kingdom shafts were re-used too (Wada 2017, 374). A few of the shaft tombs were employed for multiple burials. Burial 272/273 was a Middle Kingdom shaft tomb with two underground chambers and was used in the early 18th Dynasty again. Remains of 13 people were found, but just a few pottery vessels, some beads and a scarab with the throne name of Amenhotep I (1514–1494 BC) (Engelbach 1923, LXIII). The late 18th Dynasty seems to be missing (Wada 2007, 275). Few Ramesside objects were found (tombs 355, 387, 517, 554, 556 compare also the Ramesside stela, Engelbach 1923, pl. LXXVI, 1) and it is possible that the cemetery was still used later too.

Riqqeh: this is an umbrella name for a series of burial grounds, most likely of a provincial capital, perhaps Semenuher. Burials of the late Old Kingdom up to the Late Period were found. The burial grounds were already heavily looted when excavations started. Most New Kingdom burials are surface graves. The excavator Engelbach described several cemeteries with many simple graves. In his tomb register, he mainly published undisturbed burials, most of them again simply surface burials with a few shaft tombs, but even the shafts are not very deep. Some burials contained pottery coffins (Engelbach, Reginald 1915, 4–10, pls. XLIX–XL).

Gurob: in the cemeteries of Gurob a high number of simple surface burials were excavated, about 80 per cent of the total (Wada 2007, 358; Brunton, Engelbach 1927, 9–7, pls. XIV–CXVIII). In the New Kingdom, Gurob was the location of a palace and perhaps of a small town too. Unlike the burials of the earlier periods mentioned above, the people buried here in the New Kingdom would have belonged to a more urban environment with connection to the royal court. Burial goods of the wealthier burials show this connection.

Qau, Badari: the Qau/Badari region is up to the mid-18th Dynasty one of the major sources for burials of the wider population within a province. A certain number of burials and tombs might belong to local officials, but in general most burials are rather simple. About 160 burials are dated by Guy Brunton to the New Kingdom, mainly to the 18th Dynasty. Most of them are simple shaft tombs, some are surface burials. Many burials are placed into older tombs. Those burials next to the ancient town of Qau would belong to the population of this provincial centre. Coffins are common; most of them, perhaps even all, were rectangular boxes (Brunton 1930, 13–18, pls. XXII–XXIII).

Finally, scattered single or small surface burials dating to the New Kingdom or other periods are common at many sites and are mentioned and described sporadically. Sometimes a random selection of finds is presented in the excavation reports. Here, a small collection of such burials will be provided.

Southern pyramid at Mazghuneh: the robbed burials contained pottery and scarabs. One intact grave of a middle-aged man was found in a rough wooden coffin. The only burial good was a small wooden box containing gaming pieces (Petrie, Wainwright, Mackay 1912, 49).

Saqqara: most of Saqqara was likely covered with burials belonging to the population of Memphis. These burials are only infrequently described in excavation reports. Some examples should be mentioned here. Many burials were found over and around the remains of the 13th Dynasty pyramid of king Khendjer at Saqqara South. The burials are not presented in detail within the excavation report, but in a summary chapter Jéquier (1933, 44) explicitly calls them poor (*'pauvres'*) and wonders whether these are the burials of the inhabitants of Memphis. The bodies were not mummified. Often, several bodies were placed within one simple, rectangular wooden coffin. Burial goods include pottery, personal adornments, a few amulets. Stone vessels appear too (Jéquier 1933, 43–48, pls. X, XXI). Similar examples of burials are known from the area of Pepy's II pyramid (Jéquier 1940, 44–46).

Amarna: since 2006, several burial grounds evidently belonging to the 'common' people of Amarna have been under excavation. These results are of special importance as all graves were carefully recorded, including those with no burial goods, providing the full range of burials at a given time at a specific place, a level of detail that is otherwise very rarely encountered in Egyptian archaeology. It has been calculated that the cemeteries so far known contained about 10,000 to 13,000 rather simple burials (Stevens 2017, 112). The cemeteries seem to cover, fairly well, the whole population of the city (Stevens 2017, 110). Most often, simple surface burials were found. Multiple burials within one pit were common. Chamber tombs are also attested but not yet well researched

(Stevens 2020). Some decorated coffins were found, but overall they are rare. The same applies for stelae. Social differences are visible between the burial grounds.

The South Tombs cemetery consisted mainly of pit tombs. Three hundred and eighty-one burials were excavated between 2006 and 2013. Burials of male and female adults, as well as those of children, were found. Bodies were wrapped in matting a few times, coffins of different materials are attested. In most instances, the pits closely fit the coffins or bodies and were evidently dug shortly before the burial. The rare burial goods include pottery, personal adornments and amulets. Burials were marked with stones, there were perhaps some simple mud-brick structures and a few stelae were found.

The North Tombs cemetery shows a different profile of people buried here. They are all young, between seven and twenty-five years old at the age of death and most are women. There is not much sign of elaborate care about the bodies of these young people. No wooden coffins are attested and burial goods are much rarer in comparison to the South Tombs cemetery. It seems that often several bodies were just dropped into pits. Anna Stevens wonders whether these were workers, living and working apart from families. When they died there was no close family member left to take care of them. Burial goods are very few but include in one undisturbed burial, no. 1160, a necklace of glass and faience beads; one of the beads has a gold leaf finish (Stevens, Dabbs 2017, 137–49).

The results of the ongoing Amarna excavations are not yet fully published, so it is hard to make precise comparisons with other cemeteries. However, the burials seem most likely to belong to the broader population of Amarna, from the poorest in the North Tombs cemetery to people with some resources who could afford decorated coffins and even decorated stelae. The burials were found heavily looted, but it seems that burial goods were in general rare (Kemp 2013, 262). Pottery vessels, personal adornments and amulets are the most common items. The excavation and evaluation of these cemeteries should put an end to any discussion about whether the working population had burials. There can be little doubt that these are the burials of Amarna's broader population.

Tell el-Daba'a: this is the site of the Hyksos capital in the Second Intermediate Period. In the New Kingdom the same area became again an important city. This was the place of Pi-Ramesse, the capital of Egypt under Ramses II (1279–1213 BC). In 2005 a Ramesside Period cemetery with 127 burials was excavated and well recorded (Hulková 2013). It was found over the remains of an early 18th Dynasty palace. Most graves were simple surface burials. There is little evidence for any tomb architecture. Organic preservation is very limited. There were four clusters of burials, perhaps belonging to different families. Three of these groups included two pottery coffins, and one group had four. Some burials contained pottery vessels and some personal adornments. Most burials had no coffins. It seems that they were once wrapped in linen or reed mats but only very few remains were found. The heads were mostly oriented to the northwest. Arms were placed along the body. Children were often laid to rest in vessels. Beads and scarabs are attested. They are more common in burials of children and women. In several burials simple clay shabti figures were found, all of them uninscribed (though decoration in paint might not survive in the wet ground). Less common are clay figures of naked women lying on a bed. The social status of the people buried here is unknown. In the publication it was proposed that they had a rather 'low' social status, based on the absence of costly burial goods. Even the pottery coffins are rather simple, indicating that they were also rather cheap (Hulková 2013, 105). However, pottery coffins most likely needed some resources and so at least some people buried here had sufficient means to obtain them (Galal, Aston 2003, 174–5).

Semna: burials found in Nubia might provide another idea of what happened to many less well-to-do people after they died. Near the fortress of Semna were found several burial grounds. The largest cemetery (S 500) consisted of several rock-cut chambers, most often reached via a staircase. There were also many simple surface burials. The chambers were most likely cut in the Middle Kingdom or Second Intermediate Period, while the surface burials belong to the New Kingdom. The chambers were still used in the New Kingdom and were crammed to the ceiling with bodies and burial goods. In one tomb, sixteen burials were found (Dunham, Janssen 1960, 74, 101–2) (compare p. 70).

3 Space: Tombs and Graves
3.1 Cemeteries

Egypt is located within the Sahara, the largest desert on Earth. Agriculture is only possible along the river Nile, that flows from the south to the north and in some larger oases in the western desert. In the north, the Nile divides into several branches forming the Delta. Once a year the Nile rises, flooding the fertile lands. Most ancient settlements were therefore built on small 'islands' that were in the flood plain but not covered by the flood water. Settlements were less often placed at the edge of the desert, as there the water supply is deficient in many locations. Cemeteries were most often excavated by archaeologists in the low desert, the part closer to the cultivation. This provided, for much too long, the impression that this was the most common burial ground for ancient Egyptians. Furthermore, preservation conditions in the low desert are often good. They are a perfect target for excavations that aim for many objects, including items in organic materials. In contrast, burial grounds in the flood plain near ancient settlements are often buried several metres deep under the modern fields. They are hard to reach, often lying now under modern houses, adding further complications to reach them. However, excavations at settlement sites clearly show that a high number of ancient burials were close to settlements and towns. The clearest example is Edfu. Here were uncovered parts of the ancient town, including the town wall. Just beyond that wall, there is a cemetery dating to the late Old Kingdom and Second Intermediate Period up to the early New Kingdom. The area was packed with tombs of different types. To the Old Kingdom belong several mastabas and there were many surface burials and also many burials in mud-brick built chambers, especially in the Second Intermediate Period. A similar situation is visible for the Old Kingdom on Elephantine, where the cemeteries are also very close to the town on the same island (Seidlmayer 2006).

The evidence for the New Kingdom is similar, but not so clear. There are not so many towns excavated and organic settlements are basically still missing. At Amarna, the burials of the broader population were about 3 km east of the living quarters of the city (Stevens 2017, 121). At Amara in Nubia, cemeteries were again very close to the town (Spencer 2009). Also the New Kingdom cemeteries at Qau were quite near the ancient town, in this case in the lower desert (Seidlmayer 1990, 207). At Deir el-Medineh the burials are right next to the settlement. At Bubastis in the Delta, the burials grounds are close to the town and almost a part of it (el-Sawi 1979). At Tell el-Dab'a, New Kingdom burials were found at some distance from the centre of the Pi-Ramesse, in an area with no New Kingdom activities. Lucia Hulková, who published the cemetery, wonders whether there was a poorer suburb of Pi-Ramesse nearby (Hulková 2013, 10–11).

Burials of very young children are a problem in archaeology. Death at childbirth was most likely very common but those very young children do not appear often in cemeteries. There is some evidence for special burial grounds for babies. Baby burials within settlements are also attested (Zillhardt 2009).

In contrast, tombs of people with substantial resources could be built at a considerable distance from the next settlement. This is evident at Thebes, where kings and some high officials were buried in the Valley of the Kings, far apart from the city. At other places monumental tomb chapels were carved into the rocks at prestigious locations again far removed from the nearest town. An example is the series of the early New Kingdom rock-cut tombs near Edfu. They are some kilometres away from the town (Davies 2013, 62, fig. 1). This is in clear contrast to the Old Kingdom where the mastabas of important people stood right next to the city walls (Seidlmayer 1990, 40).

The organisation of cemeteries is often hard to follow as so few were excavated on a bigger scale. In the Ramesside burial ground at Tell el-Dab'a tombs were arranged in groups with two burials with pottery coffins in the middle. Pottery coffins were most likely quite expensive. These groups might form families or even whole households, with master and wife in the middle and servants around it (Hulková 2013, 21–32). In the tomb complex of the high steward of Amun with the name Amenemipet (TT41), at Thebes, was found a separate burial chamber with four coffins, one of which belonged to a headman of a production place, most likely working on the estate of the high steward. Amenemipet was buried with some members of his working staff (Polz 1991). However, to complicate matters, it is possible that these four people were family members of Amememipet also working on his estate. Nevertheless burials of minor officials and servants around the chapel of a master are a fairly common pattern in Ancient Egypt. At Amarna, the rock-cut tombs of the highest court officials were carved into the mountains, east of the city. There was a separate cemetery with shaft and chamber tombs, most likely belonging to people on the social level just under the court officials. The main burial grounds for the working population and some wealthier people are in the desert between the city and the mountains in the east (Stevens 2017). At Riqqeh the funerary landscape stretched over a wider area in the western low desert. At its southern end were found bigger New Kingdom burials with underground chambers, one belonging to the local governor Ipy who lived in the Amarna Period. Simpler burials, often in pottery coffins and within small brick chambers, were found north of it, along the area of cultivation (Engelbach 1915, 4–11).

In the Southern Levant, burials were often close to the settlements, sometimes on the slopes of the hills where the town or village was placed. Burials within a settlement are common too, as for example at Megiddo (Philipp 1938, Prell 2019, 139–43).

3.2 Multiple Burials

The single burial is the most common type, however, in many periods of Egyptian history it was frequent to place more than one body into a grave (Miniaci 2019). Up to the Middle Kingdom that might mainly have been done when more than one person died at about the same time. It seems that burial chambers were only opened on one occasion. This changed in the late Middle Kingdom, when there is clear evidence that burial chambers were opened more than once to place further bodies into an already existing burial space. This is best attested in the underground galleries next to the pyramid of king Senusret

III at Dahshur, where royal women were buried most likely over a greater span of time (Grajetzki 2007, 24).

This custom of multiple burials appears from the late Middle Kingdom onwards in all parts of the country, but single burials are still well attested and are the most common burial form (compare Amarna, Stevens 2017, 110–12). In the New Kingdom, both patterns existed side by side. However, a true new form of burial in the New Kingdom is those with couples, a husband and a wife (Grajetzki 2007, 29–30). This is more than once well attested due to inscriptions and it seems plausible for other burials where a body of a man is placed next to a woman. However, the custom is mainly attested for wealthier people who had the resources for a proper burial chamber. For example, at the New Kingdom cemetery at Riqqeh, this pairing is only twice attested (Engelbach 1915, pl. XLIV, tombs 86 and 296). Both cases were found in shaft tombs and one wonders whether these couples died at about the same time.

The reason for these multiple burials has not often been discussed (Miniaci 2019). Certainly changes in society and religious beliefs are one reason. In recent times it has been suggested that these might be connected with ancestor worship (Nyord 2017, 349). Family members wanted to be close to each other. However, the custom might also have had a very practical reason. It was seen as important to place the dead in a sort of cave, a place not invaded by sand. This security was given within a coffin and with a separate burial chamber. People with few resources could do that only by using already existing space. Several poorer people might have opted to combine their resources to be buried in one coffin together, providing at least some protection. Indeed, in the early New Kingdom there appears the well-attested custom of placing several bodies in one coffin. The latter custom seems to be very typical for the first half of the 18th Dynasty and is much less often attested later. The shape of coffins might be one reason. In the 18th Dynasty, rectangular boxes are most common. If they were bigger, they were suitable for more than one body. In the later New Kingdom, mummiform coffins appear all around the country. Here it was more complicated to place more than one body in them. However, even for mummiform coffins, examples containing several bodies are attested (Firth, Gunn 1926, 79–80, fig. 82 (tomb NE. 89)).

A striking example for a place with many burials is the find known as the tomb of Maket at Lahun. In three larger underground chambers were found twelve mostly rectangular coffins each filled with up to five or even six bodies (Petrie 1891, 21–4).

In the Levant, there is a long tradition of multiple burials. The dead were often placed into natural rock chambers that were enlarged or reworked to make them suitable for the bodies of the dead and their goods. These chambers often contained, when excavated, a mix of bones and burial goods, most often pottery but also personal adornments and other items (Gonen 1992, 9–15). In the Southern Levant there appears also the custom to place more than one body into a coffin, attested mainly for pottery coffins (Pouls Wegner 2015, 303–4).

3.3 Tomb Architecture

The tomb architecture in Egypt varied heavily across the different regions of the country and most importantly, from the ground available and the resources of the tomb owner. The tombs of the ruling class consisted most often of two parts. There is frequently a chapel at ground level where the cult of the dead was performed, and there was the underground burial chamber, closed at some point forever, while the cult chapel remained open to the living. The most famous cult chapels in the New Kingdom are the Theban rock-cut chapels, often decorated with paintings or reliefs showing the deceased, his family, offerings, but also daily life scenes. In the Ramesside Period, scenes showing rituals or the deceased making offerings to deities dominate. These tombs were cut into the desert rock. They often have prestigious positions overlooking the Nile valley.

Decorated chapels are not only found at Thebes, but are also known from other places in Upper Egypt, such as Qubbet el-Hawa (near Elephantine), Elkab, Hierakonpolis and Naqada. They are not yet attested for the early 18th Dynasty north of Naqada, though the rock-cut tomb of Nehesy at Saqqara dated under the ruling queen Hatshepsut (1479–1458 BC), might be cited as exception (Zivie 2003, 22). In the Ramesside Period, monumental tombs of the ruling class appear all over Egypt. It seems that there was a tendency, at least for some very high officials, to be buried at their home town. At Bogga, about 30 km south of Philae in Lower Nubia, were erected several decorated chapels; one belongs to the 'steward of the queen' Nakhtmin (Hermann 1935). At Mostagedda there was the monumental tomb of the 'overseer of the treasury' Suty, at Rifeh, a big rock-cut tomb datable under Ramses III (1187–1157 BC) (Petrie 1907, 23–24, pls. XXVIII–XXX), and near Asyut the burial of the 'overseer of the granaries' Saaset. To the late Ramesside Period belong the chapels of Pennut at Aniba (Fig. 2) and Setau at Elkab. These are just a few examples from a wider trend (Auenmüller 2014, especially pp. 181–2).

The rock-cut chapels belonged to the wealthiest people. More common in the 18th Dynasty were probably mud-brick built chapels. They often had a court at the front and were also most likely decorated with paintings. Many examples might have had a small pyramid too. As these mud-brick structures are often not

Figure 2 The tomb of Pennut at Aniba. It is an example of a decorated Ramesside tomb chapel. The scenes show Pennut in front of gods (top), family members (middle and bottom right) and a life event, Pennut receiving honours (photos: Wikicommons, Olaf Tauch, plan of tomb chapel: author)

well preserved, the paintings are only known from a few better-recorded examples (Minault-Gout, Thill 2012, 7–14, 69, pl. 20). Such chapels are well attested at Thebes (Polz 1995, passim, especially fig 1 on p. 209), but most examples were excavated in Nubia (Minault-Gout, Thill 2012, 7–14, pls. 10–50), providing the impression that they were typical for this Egyptian province. In fact they might have been equally popular all over Egypt, but are just not so well preserved at other places.

The most elaborate free-standing funerary chapels were excavated at Saqqara (Staring 2015). They most often appear as monumental, stone-built versions of the mud-brick chapels. The largest ones looked like small temples with several columned courtyards at the front and chapels for the stela of the deceased at the back. Similar elaborate tomb chapels existed at Sedment, where there were excavated the remains of the one belonging to the vizier Rahotep (Franzmeier 2017a, 308–9). His monumental tomb once had a temple-like cult chapel above ground, adorned with reliefs in different types of stone. Similar remains of the same period have been found at Gurob (Brunton, Engelbach 1927, 11, pl. XIX, tomb 36, 37) and Abydos (Randall-MacIver, Mace 1902, pls. XXVI–XXVI).

It remains unknown how the burials of the working population were marked on the surface. At Amarna were remains of loose stone settings (Stevens 2017, 106) and one wonders whether similar arrangements were typical for other cemeteries too. It seems likely that surface burials had some markers above ground, as they normally do not cut into each other when they are of about the same age (compare the plan of the cemeteries at Qau, Brunton 1930, pl. I), while it is common that later burials cut into those of much older periods.

Evidently better preserved are the underground parts of tombs and graves (Fig. 3). The simplest versions are surface burials, just placed into the sand. This was surely the most common arrangement found in all parts of Egypt and Nubia. More elaborate versions had brick walls forming small chambers (compare the typology of burials in Gurob Brunton 1927, pl. XVIII).

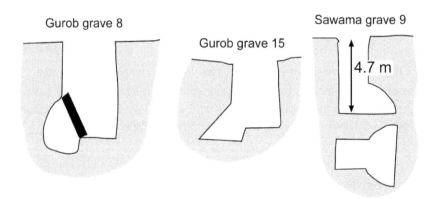

Gurob grave 8

Gurob grave 15

Sawama grave 9

4.7 m

Figure 3 Shaft tombs with small chamber, Gurob 8 and Gurob 15 (redrawn from Petrie Museum tomb card) Sawama 9 (redrawn by author from Bourriau, Millard 1971, fig. 8)

More resources (most likely mainly in time) were needed for shafts, cut a few metres deep into the ground. They are again attested in almost all parts of the country. The condition of the ground was evidently an important factor. In rocky desert ground, such burials were hard to cut but were quite stable. In sandy ground such shafts are often brick-lined to provide some stability. The next step in expenditure would be shafts with a chamber. They are again attested in most parts of the country. Here again, the ground played an important role in how these were arranged in practical terms. Where there was solid rock, the chambers had to be carved into the stone, which would require substantial extra resources. These chambers were often just big enough to contain one body. Other chambers were bigger and could host several bodies. In regions with soft ground, burial chambers could be built up of mud-bricks. Well recorded examples come from Fadrus and Tombos (Smith 2003, 142–5, fig. 6.9) in Nubia. The most complex arrangements have several underground chambers cut into the ground. Those are common at Thebes and Saqqara but rare at other places, though they were also recorded at Abydos (Garstang 1900, pl. XXXIII) and at Sedment where several such tombs can be assigned to the highest officials of the state, notably the vizier Parahotep (Petrie; Brunton 1924, pl. LXXXIV; Franzmeier 2014, fig. 4).

In the Southern Levant, many local variations are visible (Gonen 1992, 10, table 1). Burial customs in the coast regions were different to those in the mountain regions in the Southern Levant. Simple surface burials were most common, but natural caves were popular too. They were often adjusted for burials. There are several caves with carved benches. Caves are most often used for multiple burials, while surface burials are mostly reserved for single inhumations. There is not much evidence for superstructures, but as many caves were used over longer periods, some markers must have existed. From Deir el-Balaḥ, right next to the (modern) Egyptian border are known four Egyptian style stelae with Egyptian inscriptions (Ventura 1987). They were most likely tomb markers, but their original context is lost. They look very similar to the stelae found at Amarna (Kemp 2013, 259, fig. 7.32).

4 Burial Goods: Daily Life versus Objects of Funerary Industry

What type of objects went into a burial in the New Kingdom? A tomb like that of King Tutankhamun (1334–24 BC) might provide the impression that next to many ritual items, the whole contents of the palace were crammed into his relatively small burial chambers. However, the items placed into burials of the wider population were quite restricted and most likely had special functions within the burial or in rituals performed at the mummification and at the funeral.

Several previous researches investigated the burial goods of New Kingdom
graves. The initial major study comes from Stuart Tyson Smith (1992) who
compared several undisturbed New Kingdom Theban tombs and divided the
types of objects into different categories. His main division is between 'objects
for the tomb' and 'objects of daily life'. In a later study, Smith (2003, 143–66)
distinguished between 'objects designed for the tomb' and 'objects of daily
life', to evaluate the cemeteries of Fadrus (Nubia), Harageh, Qau and Gurob. In
all these cemeteries, specialised funerary items are rather rare. Even at Gurob,
a burial place for some higher officials, only about 10 per cent of the burials
contained them. Franzmeier distinguishes in his evaluation of the New
Kingdom cemeteries at Sedment, four types of objects: funeralia, objects of
daily use, objects belonging to both types and tools for building the tombs or for
placing burial goods into the burial chamber (Franzmeier 2017a, 333). By
funeralia, Franzmeier means objects especially made for the tomb. In
a statistical evaluation, he shows that about 35 per cent of objects found in the
cemeteries of Sedment were daily life objects, 55 per cent funeralia and the rest
not identifiable (Franzmeier 2017a, 342). The high proportion of funeralia in the
Sedment burials contrasts heavily with the low quantity of funeralia at Fadrus,
Qau, Harageh and Gurob, investigated by Smith. However, these statistics for
Sedment include burials of all periods within the New Kingdom, while burials
at Fadrus, Qau and Harageh mainly belong to the 18th Dynasty. Looking at the
two periods separately, a different picture emerges. In the 18th Dynasty, only
about 13.5 per cent of the objects in burials were funeralia, while this was
85.2 per cent in the Ramesside Period (datings based on Sedment, Franzmeier
2017a, table 7.6 on p. 343).

Further classifications of burial goods applied to New Kingdom cemeteries at
Nubia deliver similar results. Williams (1992, 98–132) makes the following
categorisation for a series of smaller burial grounds at Qustul: the funeralia are
mainly coffins and shabtis. All further objects found might be rather classified
as daily life objects. There are some remains of furniture, most importantly
headrests, but also ivory inlays perhaps from boxes. A high percentage of daily
life objects are cosmetic items. There are kohl tubes, stone vessels and boxes for
holding tweezers, mirrors, razors and trimmers. Most common were the personal adornments, including many beads, scarabs and amulets, although many
amulets might be classified as funeralia too. Other object types were rather rare.
There was one axe and a fish hook. Eight metal vessels were found; due to the
high material value of these objects, many more might have been originally
deposited in these graves.

A similar arrangement of objects appears in the publication of tombs from Sai
(Nubia; Minault-Gout Thill 2012). The material found in the burials is separated

into funeralia, personal adornments, cosmetic objects, pottery, terracotta figures, non-ceramic vessels, tools and objects made of bone, ivory and wood. From the remains it is clear that some high status people were buried at Sai. The funeralia include a wide range of objects: coffins, mummy masks, miniature canopic jars, shabtis made of different materials, heart scarabs and model scribal palettes (Minault-Gout Thill 2012, 164–229).

Combining the evidence for those particular cemeteries, there are three dominant objects groups that appear repeatedly in the burials of the New Kingdom. These are the objects made for the burial, the pottery vessels and personal including cosmetic objects. The objects made for the burial are more common in cemeteries of the Ramesside Period and, unsurprisingly, in cemeteries with many people belonging to the ruling class.

4.1 Body Protection, Coffins and Mummy Masks

In the New Kingdom bodies of the deceased were most often placed on their back with the arms stretched out along the body. The head was most often oriented to the west, towards the Underworld. However, there are many exceptions to this rule (Raven 2005, 52; Hulková 2013, 35–9). At Amarna, no clear rule in orientation is visible (Stevens 2017, 120). In contrast, at Fadrus in Nubia, bodies were rather oriented to the east (Spence 2019, 546). At Qustul and Adindan, also in Nubia, most bodies were oriented to the west or east, with some exceptions (Williams 1992, 21). At Tell el Farah, in the Southern Levant, half of the bodies were oriented to the south (Braunstein 2011, 22).

The cheapest way to protect a body would be to place it in a mat (Fig. 4). At places with good organic preservation conditions, matting is often mentioned as device for wrapping up bodies (compare the tomb register for Gurob, Brunton, Engelbach 1927, pls. XIV–XVIII). Baskets as body container are another option for less wealthy people (Brunton, Engelbach 1927, p. XIV, tomb 25), but seem to be not very common.

Simple wooden coffins are the next level of expenditure. It is hard to say how expensive plain wooden coffins were. In the South Tombs Cemetery at Amarna, they appear in about 5 per cent of the burials. The North Tombs Cemetery did not contain a single coffin (Stevens 2017, 109, 117).

The development of coffin styles is easiest to follow at Thebes, whereas the coffin production at places far away from the centres of power is often hard to track, due to bad recording of the examples found. With rare exceptions, organic preservation is not always good and many coffins certainly have disappeared without trace. However, it seems clear that simple, undecorated, rectangular boxes were most common throughout the country all through the 18th Dynasty (Fig. 5),

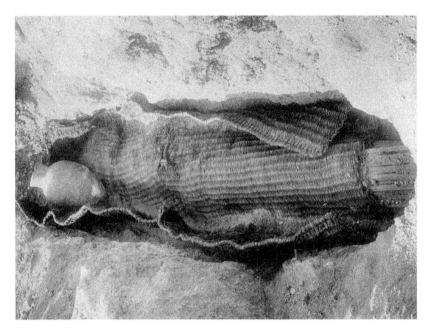

Figure 4 Burial at Gurob where a woman is wrapped in
mats (Loat 1905, 2, pl. VII, 1)

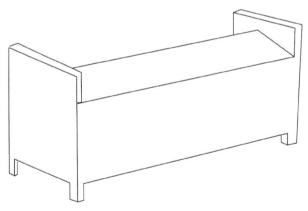

Figure 5 Undecorated wooden coffin from Sedment, tomb 254, redrawn from
tomb card (now Inventory number Cairo TR12.5.21.4; redrawn by author)

perhaps even for people with some resources. It seems that most local centres
did not have workshops for more elaborate coffins, as known from Thebes or
Saqqara (and Amarna). Simple boxes are often mentioned in excavation
reports, but rarely recorded so that even technical details regarding the con-
struction are not known. At least some of them had a lid with a gable (Bruyère
1937, 32–5; Franzmeier 2017, 181). Sometimes rectangular coffin boxes were

decorated with geometric patterns, best known from the Memphite cemeteries and from Beni Hassan (Garstang 1907, 181, fig. 189). At Lahun (Petrie 1891, 22), Abydos (Grajetzki 2016) and Thebes were also found examples with figures, most often showing deities, sometimes accompanied by short inscriptions (Bruyère 1929, 35–44; further examples listed in Grajetzki 2016, 56).

At the end of the Middle Kingdom coffin production had changed radically, with the appearance of mummiform coffins (Grajetzki 2010). In the Middle Kingdom, rectangular coffins of the ruling class were often decorated with long religious texts, called Coffin Texts, there are friezes of objects used in rituals and long offering lists naming mainly foods for eternal nourishment. The outsides of these coffins are most often decorated with text columns and text lines. In the late Middle Kingdom (about 1850 to 1650 BC) the inside decoration of coffins disappears. It was no longer seen as important to place religious texts or depictions of ritual objects there. The outside decoration did not change much, but over time it seems that decorated coffins became rarer and were mostly restricted to centres with royal connections, such as the Memphis-Fayum region, Abydos and Thebes. At other places, decorated coffins are extremely rare within the Second Intermediate Period. In this period the royal court moved to Thebes, where there developed a new coffin type, known in Egyptology as the rishi coffin (Miniaci 2011). These are mummy-shaped boxes decorated with a feather decor (*rishi* is the Arabic word for 'feathered'). Mummy-shaped coffins existed already in the Middle Kingdom but were always part of a set and always the inner coffin. In contrast, rishi coffins were not part of a coffin set. They are mainly restricted to Thebes and are evidently a product of Theban funerary culture. Rishi coffins were still being produced in the early 18th Dynasty. Next to these mummy-shaped rishi coffins were also produced coffins without any decoration, similar in design to the rishi coffins but lacking the distinctive feather decoration (Miniaci 2011, 26, fig. 21).

New Kingdom
The early 18th Dynasty also sees the appearance of a new type of coffin with white background and painted, colourful scenes (Fig. 6, top left). These are rarely seen outside of Thebes, though there are also some examples from Saqqara (Fig. 7) (Grajetzki 2003, cover). Furthermore, some mummy-shaped coffins are also attested in the early 18th Dynasty at provincial sites. Some of those examples look rather clumsy (for example, the coffin of Tarenu from Sedment, Miniaci 2011, 147, fig. 157; coffins in the tomb of Maket at Lahun, Petrie 1891, 22) giving the impression that the local workshops did not yet really know how to make those coffins. Under Hatshepsut (1479–1458 BC), coffins with a black background became the dominant format for the ruling class

Figure 6 Coffins from Thebes (left to right), Hormose, 'white coffin', early
18th Dynasty, New York, MA Rogers fund 36.3.172; Khonsu, 'yellow coffin',
19th Dynasty; New York, MA 86.1.2a. bottom: 'black coffin' (from T. M. Davis,
The Tomb of Iouiya and Touiya, London, Archibald Constable & Co. Ltd.1907, pl. VII).

Figure 7 White coffin found at Saqqara, early 18th Dynasty. (Munro excavations 1995–6 near Unas pyramid causeway). The coffin contained next to the body of the deceased a set of musical instruments (photo: author).

at Thebes (Fig. 6, bottom). They have a highly standardised decoration pro-gramme, showing several Underworld deities with spells all relating to rituals at mummification. These coffins have been found throughout Egypt, including at the Fayum, and at Amarna, as well as at several cemeteries in Nubia (Randall-Maciver, Woolley, Leonard 1911, 141; Williams 1992, 90). They are still well attested in the Ramesside Period (Sartini 2015). Finally, at the end of the 18th Dynasty appear coffins with a yellow background (Niwiński 1988, 12; Ikram, Dodson 1998, 214) (Fig. 6, top right). So far those coffins are best attested at Thebes. Depictions of the deceased in front of different deities are common on the lid. They are well attested in the Ramesside Period too. In the late 18th Dynasty coffins showing the deceased in a festival dress also became popular (Niwiński 1988, 12–13). The earliest example is perhaps the sarcophagus of the 'high steward' Iniuia, under Tutankhamun (Schneider, 2012, 109–15). Many more examples in wood are known from Thebes and the Memphite region. Those in the Memphite region were often found buried in the sand (Borchardt 1909, 74–5), indicating that these coffins were also used by people not belonging to the wealthiest social level. Under the reign of Amenhotep III (1390–1353 BC), mummy-shaped sarcophagi became common in burials for the highest state officials. Under Ramses II they are found in most parts of Egypt and Nubia, but mostly at Thebes and Saqqara (Böhme 2019). Very few examples are datable after Ramses II. Within the New Kingdom also appear pottery coffins (Cotelle-Michel 2004), that are again vaguely mummy shaped although the modelling of face and arms is often rough. They are known mainly from the northern parts of Egypt, but appear in Nubia too. They are also well attested in the Southern Levant (van den Brink, et al., 2017, 126–8). Well-made examples are often painted and inscribed (Cotelle-Michel 2004, 232–3, Kat II-B1-1). It seems certain that they already belonged to people with a higher level of resources (Galal, Aston 2003, 174–5).

The coffin production for the broader population of the Ramesside Period is surprisingly elusive. Many burials without any signs of coffins were found at Gurob. In several burials mats were used and several burials had mud-brick built coffins in vaguely mummiform shape (Brunton 1930, pl. XVIII, type A). Many burials without coffins also emerge when looking at the Ramesside cemetery at Tell el-Dab'a. Here some pottery coffins were found; children were often placed into pottery vessels, but there are no signs of wooden coffins for most of the adults (Hulková 2013, 27). With all due reservation, it might be argued that coffins lost importance.

Figure 8 Miniature mummy mask, Rifeh, tomb 168, Petrie Museum, London UC 72746 (Courtesy of the Petrie Museum, UCL)

Mummy masks

In the early New Kingdom, tiny mummy masks (Fig. 8) appear mainly in Upper Egypt (summary Casini 2017; Rogge 1988a, 1988b; further examples Abydos: Garstang 1900, pl. xviii), but only for the wealthiest people. For example, in the New Kingdom cemeteries at Qau/Badari, only one mask is recorded (Brunton 1930, 15). About ten masks were found in the smaller cemeteries at Rifeh, perhaps not so much indicating different local customs as providing evidence that the cemeteries excavated at Rifeh belong to a wealthier social level. Masks are also well attested at Nubian sites such as Fadrus (Säve-Söderbergh, Troy 1991, 64–75), Aniba (Näser 2017, 563–4) and Buhen (Randall-Maciver, Woolley, Leonard 1911, 138, 142, 173, 177, 145, pls. 60–1). Most often just the plaster face is preserved, but not the cartonnage (a material made of linen or papyrus covered with plaster and then painted). However, at Beni Hasan one example survived in good condition, showing a tiny face and a huge headdress (Garstang 1907, 177, fig. 183, see also Ikram, Dodson 1998, 169, fig. 196). The examples just described belong to the Second Intermediate Period and early New Kingdom, while mummy masks appear later only sporadically. They are known from the highest social level (Tutankhamun (KV62) or Maiperheri (KV36)), but are not as regular as in the Middle Kingdom when they were common in almost all burials that also had a decorated coffin. However, in many provincial cemeteries of the early New Kingdom they are the only objects especially made for the grave, apart from the undecorated coffins.

Mummification

Finally, some remarks should be made about mummification and the treatment of the body. There is little doubt that in the 18th Dynasty the royal family and most higher officials received some form of treatment that can be classified as mummification (list of royal mummies of the 18th Dynasty: Ikram, Dodson 1998, 321–5). Herodotus (*Histories* II, chapters 86–8) described the procedure of mummification that includes removing the brain and the entrails, and placing the body for seventy days into natron. However, little is known about what happened with the bodies of the mass of the population. Here detailed research on bodies found in provincial cemeteries is missing. Smith refers to Herodotus and noted that in the wealthiest Theban burials he investigated, two types of mummification are visible: the full set including the use of canopic jars for the entrails, but also a cheaper version, where there were no canopic jars (Smith 1992, 199).

Wrappings and linen are often mentioned in excavation reports but it remains unclear whether these wrapped bodies received any treatment that can be classified as 'mummification'. Canopic jars and canopic boxes are not often attested at provincial cemeteries of the 18th Dynasty. This might already indicate that mummification as known from the higher officials at Thebes was not so common. A well-preserved mummy was found at Sedment in an early 18th Dynasty mummiform coffin of Tarenu (compare p. 31; Serpico 2008, 136 (with photo); Franzmeier 2017b, 384). This is one of the very few coffins of this type from this period outside of Thebes and points to the high social status of this woman. However, the body of this woman was never analysed, so it remains unclear whether she was properly mummified (as described by Herodotus) or whether the body survived well due to the dry climate at Sedment. This is a problem that holds true for most burials known from old excavations.

4.1.2 Other Objects Made For the Burial

Canopic jars and canopic boxes are common in wealthier tombs at Thebes from the early 18th Dynasty on (Smith 1992, 199). They are also attested in Saqqara for the 18th Dynasty and appear sporadically at other sites at the same time, such as Sedment (Franzmeier 2017a, 187–8). Otherwise, they are not common in the provinces. Not one is known from the New Kingdom cemeteries at Riqqeh or Harageh; in Gurob some are attested for the Ramesside Period (Brunton, Engelbach 1927, 15, 20).

Perhaps the most famous object made for the burial, however, is the Book of the Dead. These are papyri containing liturgies, providing the deceased with guidance and help to the Underworld. Most of these papyri also have images providing visual aid. Many spells of the Book of the Dead are already known in the Middle Kingdom, but only within the Second Intermediate Period, it seems they were put together in specific sequences (Dorman 2017, 34), that also often appear on the later Book of the Dead papyri of the New Kingdom. This might relate to a change in afterlife beliefs and to new funeral rituals. In the early New Kingdom, these spells appear sporadically on mummy shrouds or very rarely on coffins or sarcophagi. In the mid-18th Dynasty they appear more regularly on papyri; the spells themselves are also attested on a wide range of other objects. Indeed, for many spells the Book of the Dead is just one of the places for writing these spells, such as the spells on heart scarabs (spell 30b), on shabtis (spell 6) or parts of spell 151 more commonly found on coffins. The Book of the Dead papyri are again mainly attested at Thebes and for the wealthiest people. It is hard to say how common it was at other places. There are some papyri assigned to Saqqara (Munro 1988, 272–3), but the bad preservation conditions for organic materials such as papyri makes it hard to judge how common they were there. A well-made Book of the Dead papyrus was also found at Sedment, a cemetery were several court officials were buried (Franzmeier 217b, 122).

Book of the Dead papyri are common in wealthier 18th Dynasty Theban burials and are still well attested in those of the Ramesside Period (Quirke 2013, XVI–XXIV).

4.2 Mummiform Figures/Shabties (Fig. 9)

Mummiform figures (Nyord 2018, 74–75), also often known by the Egyptian word shabti (also called shawabti or ushebti, Milde 2012, 2) emerge in the late Middle Kingdom and appear sporadically in Theban burials of the 18th Dynasty (Miniaci 2014, 260–9). Only in the 19th Dynasty do they seem to become standard in most burials of a certain level of wealth. Not all are mummiform: as with coffins some are shown in a festive dress instead (from the Amarna Period onwards). Those with a longer inscription often have a spell about freeing the

Figure 9 Shabtis (left): Bristol Museum & Art Gallery
(inv. no. H342). (right): Tomb 278 in Rifeh (Petrie Museum, London
(inv. no. UC 39779 Courtesy of the Petrie Museum, UCL); photos: author;
previously published in Grajetzki (2020b), figs. 10, 11.

deceased from corvée work in the Underworld. The shabtis of the Ramesside Period in particular vary hugely in quality. They range from palace art works to crude mould-made examples in poorer burials (Fig. 9). Some crude examples seem to be handmade. Especially the rougher examples are often made of clay and seem to be mass produced. Some of these are inscribed. It seems possible that they were affordable to a much wider range of people, including not very wealthy individuals (Poole 1999). Rough wooden examples are also common. In the less wealthy burials, these figures are most often the only grave good in the Ramesside Period. One example is a Ramesside cemetery at Bubastis with many simple burials; a few contained pottery, some personal adornments were found and several times simple pottery mummiform figures (el-Sawi 1979, 84–5). Mummiform figures appear very rarely also in burials in the Southern Levant (Eliezer 1973, 61, fig. 9, 224–229, figs. 44a-45).

4.3 Female Fertility Figures

Fertility figures of naked or almost naked women (Fig. 10) begin to appear in the archaeological records of early Middle Kingdom burials. In the Middle Kingdom they were often made of wood, in the late Middle Kingdom, faience became a common material too. Especially the faience figures are sometimes of

Figure 10 Some typical objects from 18th Dynasty burials all found at Sawama (not to scale) and now in the Brooklyn Museum (all images are Creative Commons-BY Brooklyn Museum) (top row): faience bowl, tomb 49 (no. 14.610); large vessel, tomb 91 (no. 14.642); (bottom row): faience cosmetic pot, tomb 49 (no. 14.609); necklace with silver flies, tomb 53 (no. 14.641); right: clay figure of woman on bed, tomb 102 (no. 14.608)

high artistic value. In New Kingdom burials clay, faience and stone figures of naked women, often lying on a bed, appear sporadically (Qau: Brunton 1930, pl. XXXV, 40, 46; Riqqeh: Engelbach 1915, pl. XXII, 6; Sawama: Bourriau, Millard 1971, pl. XVII, 1, fig. 19; Gurob: Brunton, Engelbach 1927, pl. XXV, 20, XLVII, 10, 15). Many of the clay examples were most likely made in moulds and resemble in terms of production simple clay shabtis. In the Ramesside Period, burial goods are in general rare, and therefore it is remarkable that these female clay figures still appear in burials, even though not as often as shabtis. They evidently had a function needed at least for some people in the afterlife, perhaps as substitutes for a caring mother or symbols of fertility (D'Auria 1988).

4.4 Pottery and Vessels of Other Materials

Pottery vessels are the most frequent burial goods (Figs 10, 11) in the archaeological record, up to the Ramesside Period, when a major change can be seen.

The function of pottery vessels within a burial is not always clear. Big storage jars might be containers for the eternal food supply. Very small vessels might be containers for perfumes, similar to small stone vessels. Small cosmetic vessels

Figure 11 Early 18th Dynasty vessel, typical for many burials of the period, provenance unknown, Petrie Museum, UC 16389 (Courtesy of the Petrie Museum, UCL); photo: author

whether made in stone or clay were evidently part of the cosmetic equipment often found in burials of women. Some vessels, particularly the open forms, seem to belong to tableware (Bourriau 1981, 72, 135 (no. 264)).

In early 18th Dynasty burials small, tall drinking vessels are very popular, indicating that many pottery sets might be a combination of tableware for a symbolic eternal meal (Helmbold-Doyé, Seiler 2019, 146). Other vessels in early New Kingdom burials might also belong to tableware such as jugs with a handle (Helmbold-Doyé, Seiler 2019, 196–7). Imported vessels, most often coming from Mycenaean Greece, are quite common, even in burials which cannot be considered very wealthy (Helmbold-Doyé, Seiler 2019, 354–400).

Other characteristic vessels of the early to mid-18th Dynasty are the so-called flower pots. They are typical for Thebes and some other sites, but do not appear everywhere in Egypt. Claudia Näser (2001, 378–9) looked at the examples found in undisturbed tombs at Deir el-Medineh at Thebes. Different types of food were found in most of them. She argues that these were vessels for food offerings presented by different people for the burial while attending the funeral. In Deir el-Medineh these vessels appear in greater numbers, providing the impression that several people connected in some way with the deceased were presenting them. At other cemeteries 'flower pots' appear more sporadically. Several examples were excavated at Saï (Budka 2017, 121, fig. 16). At Qustul, were found a number of well-preserved burials, many of which only contained one flower pot (Williams 1992, 186, 194, 207, 251, 263, 271, 303). Only in tomb VC 48 were discovered several of this vessel type (Williams 1992, 280). Its tomb chamber contained more than one burial and some high status objects, including mummiform coffins. In contrast, at the Nubian site of Aniba 175 'flower pots' were found in thirty-one burials all together. In one grave even thirty-seven of them were discovered (Helmbold-Doyé, Seiler 2019, 122). This provides the impression that burial customs at Aniba were heavily influenced by burial traditions at Thebes.

Pottery vessels become markedly rarer in burials in the course of the New Kingdom. Janine Bouriau (1981, 72) noted that under Hatshpsut (1479–1458 BC) and Thutmose III (1470–1425 BC), tableware and food containers began to disappear, while containers for cosmetics and perhaps medicaments became more common. Pottery vessels are not common in burials at Amarna. This change most likely relates to a transformation of belief systems. Those vessels found now are often large vessels for embalming materials. Food containers and tableware all but disappear. Yet even the vessels for embalming materials are not very common. However, there are still exceptions to the general patterns. Some rather simple Ramesside burials found at Tell el-Dab'a contained a single vessel, such as two burials of children with armlets made of beads, or a necklace and a beer jar next to the head (Hulková 2013, 108–10).

In the Southern Levant a similar range of vessels appears, but there are also differences from Egypt. In the Ramesside Period, there is no decline visible in the custom of placing pottery in burials. Pottery in cave tombs is often domestic and of local production (Gonen 1992, 14). In contrast pit burials often contained storage jars and a high number of imported vessels (Gonen 1992, 19–20). Lamps can appear in high numbers within burials, something not attested in Egypt to the same extent.

Susan Braunstein (2011, 21, table 8) undertook a thorough study comparing burials at Farah (Southern Levant) with those at Gurob and Matmar. Most burials at Tell el Farah contained some pottery, contrasting with only half of the graves at the Egyptian sites. Several types of pottery vessels are attested both in Egypt and Tell el Farah. These include bowls or drop-shaped jars. However, a range of other vessels is typically found only at Tell el Farah. Jugs and juglets are very common at Tell el Farah, but rare in Egypt. Pilgrim flasks also appear more often in Farah, than in Egypt. Lamps appear in 15 per cent of graves in Tell el Farah, but not at all at the selected Egyptian sites.

Imitation Vessels

In Theban burials of the 18th Dynasty there were found solid imitation vessels made of wood and then plastered and finely painted. They most often imitate different types of stone vessels but also glass ones. A high proportion is inscribed with the name of the deceased. These vessels were evidently made for the burial. Their function is enigmatic as they were mainly found in the burials of the wealthiest people. It seems implausible therefore that they represent substitutes for more expensive vessels, as wealthy people could afford the more expensive versions (Gander 2009, Gander 2012).

A different case is a small roughly made mud vessel type found in a few New Kingdom burials in many parts of Egypt. They are most often not taller than ten centimetres and are non-functional as a vessel, as they are normally not hollow (examples: Brunton 1930, pl. XXIII, tombs 5404, 5532; Bourriau, Millard 1971, 38, fig. 6, nos. 112–14, 117, 121; Engelbach 1923, pl. LXIII, tomb 363, dated under Thutmose IV (1400–1390 BC); Petrie 1907, pl. XXVIIA). Due to their limited aesthetic value it seems possible that they were slightly more common than it appears now, as they might often have gone unrecorded. Their function must remain obscure. However, tomb 7260 (Brunton 1930, 15) at Qau might give a very general clue. Here ten little pots were found about one metre above the bottom of the shaft. One wonders whether these are better-made versions of the mud examples. The find spot indicates that they might have been used in rituals at the end of the funeral. They might have been dropped into the shaft after the burial chamber was already closed and were therefore not part of the burial equipment proper.

4.5 Personal Adornments and Amulets

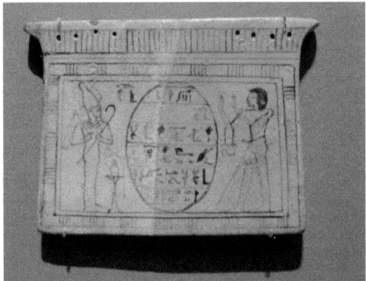

Figure 12 Two pectorals, made for burials and typical for the Ramesside period of the wealthiest people (top: Walters Art Museum 42.199 (Creative Commons), bottom: Brooklyn Museum no. 37.885E Creative Commons-BY Brooklyn Museum)

Personal adornments are well attested in 18th Dynasty burials. They include bracelets, earrings, finger rings, several types of pendants, and many beads. In contrast, broad collars are not common at all. Jewellery appears in almost all periods of Egyptian history among grave goods. Beads and amulets are frequent finds in burials of almost all social levels and still appear in the Ramesside Period when other types of objects became very rare. The dividing line between personal adornment and amulet is not always clear and might be more a modern concept. Bes and Taweret were deities especially important for protecting mother and child. Figurative pendants showing Bes or Taweret are evidently amulets and are common (Andrews 1994, 40), but a broad collar might also have had a protective function and might be classified as an amulet (Andrews 1994, 96).

Most jewellery in New Kingdom burials seems to come from daily life. There is not much evidence for the use of funerary jewellery. This is in contrast to the Middle Kingdom. In the Middle Kingdom, broad collars, armlets and anklets are typical for the wealthiest burials at the cemeteries near the royal residences, but also in the cemeteries in the provinces. There is good evidence that they were just made for the burials (Grajetzki 2014b, 129–34). Nothing on a comparable scale is known from the New Kingdom. The few examples of personal adornments made for a burial come from burials of the royal family. The clearest example is the burial of three queens of king Thutmose III (1470–1425 BC). Here were found different broad collars and other items surely just produced for the tomb (Lilyquist 2003, 129–35 (necklaces for heart scarabs, broad collars of gold sheet, golden sandals)). Many personal adornments in the royal tombs in the Valley of the Kings are certainly further examples of this type of jewellery, such as a collar with a vulture from the late 18th Dynasty tomb KV 55 (Aldred 1971, 20, 211–12, no. 72) and from the tomb of Tutankhamun (KV 62).

Amulets are certainly a separate category. In individual cases it is often hard to tell whether they are made in workshops especially for a burial or whether they were already worn in daily life. Typical and clear Ramesside examples made for the burial are rectangular-shaped pectorals often made in faience but also in other materials (Fig. 12). It might be argued that some of them might have be worn in daily life, but it seems most likely that they were made for the burial. They are most often decorated with Underworld deities, such as Anubis (Petrie 1914, 24–5 (91), pl. X). They are known from several sites around the country (Rifeh: Engelbach 1915, pl. XXII, 10–12; Sedment: Franzmeier 2017: 167–8), but again they most likely belong to wealthier people, and are accordingly more common at sites with a high number of richer burials.

Popular amulet forms are also small figurines of deities, especially showing Bes and Taweret. They appear often in burials of children, perhaps indicating the special need for protection that children have. Unsurprisingly then, five

Taweret figures and four Bes figures were found in one Ramesside burial of a child at Tell el-Daba (Hulková 2013, 78–80). To place these examples in context, few other amulets were present in this cemetery of 127 burials.

Other amulets of the Ramesside Period include heart scarabs, snake-head amulets, ankh signs, djed pillars and tiyet pillars. Heart scarabs are already known from the 13th Dynasty and appear sporadically in the 18th Dynasty. They then become more common in the Ramesside Period, but again here mostly for the wealthiest segments of society (Gurob: Petrie 1890, pl. XXIV, nos. 3, 4, 6–8; Riqqeh: Engelbach 1915, pl. XVI; common at Saï: Minault-Gout, Florence 2012, 197–227, pls 102–13).

Scarabs belong to the most frequent finds in New Kingdom graves and are still attested in Ramesside Period burials. They were most likely already used in daily life, possibly as amulets, and most likely continued to serve this purpose in burials. They are common at Gurob although fewer examples come from Ramesside burials (Brunton 1930, pls. XL–XLI). Five steatite scarabs were found in the Ramesside cemetery at Tell el-Daba, worn or held all at the left-hand side (Hulková 2013, 74–7).

4.6 Cosmetic Objects

In undisturbed Theban tombs of wealthier people, cosmetic items are very frequent (Smith 1992, 206–8). They are equally characteristic of not so well equipped burials. Typical items are stones vessels (Fig. 10), combs, mirrors, wooden kohl tubes and kohl sticks. They appear at sites throughout Egypt and Nubia, especially in burials of the 18th Dynasty. In the richest tombs, elaborate cosmetic spoons are attested too (Brunton, Petrie 1924, pl. LIV, 11, 12). Boxes for cosmetic equipment are also found not only in rich tombs (examples: Sedment: Brunton, Petrie 1924, LV, 3–4, LVII, 30, 31; Sawama: Bourriau, Millard 1971, fig. 15, tomb 80, fig. 19 ivory slips, most likely from boxes).

Cosmetic objects in Egyptian burials have a long tradition. Already in the Badarian and Naqada Periods such items were placed into burials of almost all social levels (Grajetzki 2020a, 63–4). In the classical Old Kingdom they are rare simply because it was no longer a custom to place objects into a burial. In the First Intermediate Period and Middle Kingdom they became again very common (Seidlmayer 1990, 206). The most famous examples are perhaps the jewellery and cosmetic boxes in the tomb of king's daughter Sithathoriunet at Lahun, dating to the 12th Dynasty. Her jewellery belongs to the finest ever produced in Egypt. Sets of cosmetic equipment are also still attested in the Second Intermediate Period. Small cosmetic stone vessels, kohl sticks and tweezers appear regularly in burials of the period (compare Brunton 1930, pls. V–VII, tombs 720, 902, 1305,

3763, 7143, 7352). The tradition is still well attested in the early New Kingdom (Brunton 1930, pls. XXII–XXIII, tombs 1038, 5297, compare Franzmeier 2017a, 155–64). However, at one point within the New Kingdom they seem to disappear. The exact timing of this development is unclear but relates evidently to the general disappearance of daily life objects from burials over the course of the New Kingdom.

The importance of cosmetic objects in burials is, from the archaeological evidence, unmistakable. However, the exact function of these items in burials is not so clear. Status might explain the examples found in burials of men. In burials of women they seem to confirm a gender identity. In burials of young women, they might be the equivalent of a dowry, providing a young woman with a gendered template of material thought necessary for their marriage. The objects of a dowry are listed in a papyrus found on Elephantine and dating to 449 BC: one garment of wool, a mirror, a single pair of sandals, a small quantity of castor oil and a tray (Porten 2011, 210). These items, most importantly the mirror and the oil, recall those found in many burials of women from the late Old Kingdom on to the early New Kingdom.

Figure 13 Headrest, Rifeh tomb 223, Victoria & Albert Museum, no.752&A 1907 (photo: author)

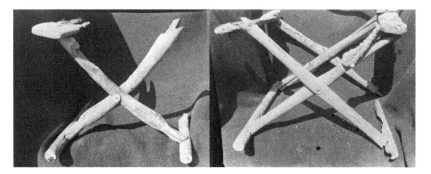

Figure 14 Two folding chairs (from Petrie 1907, pl. XXVIIB).

4.7 Furniture

Furniture is a regular feature in many 18th Dynasty Theban tombs of the wealthiest people. It is not common at all in other New Kingdom burials or in burials before the New Kingdom. The one big exception is the tomb of the king's mother Hetepheres at Giza, dating to the early Fourth Dynasty. The burial chamber of this queen, mother of Khufu, the builder of the largest pyramid at Giza, was found filled with furniture (Münch 2000). The other exceptions are the cosmetic boxes noted above as common in burials of women and in those of very wealthy men. Headrests appear in many burials of the Old and Middle Kingdom too. In Old Kingdom burials they might indicate that the person also had a headrest in daily life and was perhaps a head of a household, and there the only person with a headrest (Seidlmayer 2001, 227).

From the start of the New Kingdom, there appears in Theban tombs a full range of all types of furniture, mostly again in the burials of the most wealthy people. These include chairs, beds, tables, and a great variety of boxes (Bruyère 1929, 45–58; Smith 1992, 205–6). However, despite the many examples it seems that the furniture was not seen as essential. None was found in the burial of Maiherperi in the Valley of the Kings. This person was closely linked to the royal court (Lakomy 2016, 72–4). Outside Thebes, furniture appears too, but it is much rarer. The best preserved examples come from Beni Hasan, where in tomb 287 were found a bed and a stool (Garstang 1907, 123, 118, for the date see p. 222). A table and a chair come from tomb 183, that might date to the very early 18th Dynasty (Garstang 1907, 120, fig. 114, 122, fig. 117a). Headrests (Fig. 13) are also well attested in several provincial cemeteries, such as Rifeh (Petrie 1907, pls. XXVIIF, 172, 173, XXVIIJ (309)), Sedment (Franzmeier 2017a, 169–72) or Gurob (Brunton, Engelbach 1927, pl. XXV, 31). Most of these burials likely belong to people with some substantial resources. Simple chairs, often folding stools (Fig. 14), are found outside Thebes too (Lahun:

Petrie 1890, pl. XVIII.17; Rifeh: Petrie 1907, pl. XXVIIB), but again, these are always a few examples within larger cemeteries. Otherwise, the bulk of the population did not have any furniture in the burials. Baskets belong in a wider sense to furniture too. They were found in many burials of the 18th Dynasty and were most often used as storage devices. At Thebes, they are attested at almost all social levels (Smith 206, 1992). The reason for including furniture among the grave goods is not always clear, but ritual functions seem likely. Furniture as status marker is certainly also an additional option. In one Theban burial even model furniture was found (Bruyère 1937, 132; Näser 2013, 656).

4.8 Weapons

Weapons appear sporadically in burials of men and women. Among the finest examples are the arrows and the quiver in the tomb of Maiherperi (KV36, mid-18th Dynasty) in the Valley of the Kings (Lakomy 2016, 232–44) and those from the tomb of Tutankhamun. Daggers appear in a few burials that are otherwise not remarkable (Qau: Brunton 1930, pl. XXIII (tomb 7618)). At Riqqeh a spear head was found in one grave and an arrow head in another one (Engelbach 1915, pl. XLV (graves 422, 426)). At Qustul (Lower Nubia) there was found an axe at the pelvis of the dead in one burial (Williams 1992, 175).

A burial with bows and arrows was excavated at Saqqara, almost providing the impression that this was the burial place of a warrior (see p. 64). The function of weapons within a grave is not always clear, but there is enough evidence that axes, for example, were used as ceremonial objects (Darnell, Manassa 2007, 75–6). So they might indicate a social status and not automatically a profession. Few objects in New Kingdom burials seem to be rigidly restricted to a gender. Mirrors, hairpins and combs are more common in those of women (Smith 1992, 207–8). Weapons were perhaps more typical for men (Smith 1992, 209).

In the Southern Levant, weapons seem to be a fairly standard choice of items for burials (Gonen 1992, 15, 45, 52; Prell 2019, 130–8). They are often connected with male burials but due to bad preservation and recording of the skeletons this is most often just speculation. In the burials at Megiddo, to give one example, weapons were common and included spearheads, daggers, knife blades and axe heads (Guy 1938, 163–8).

4.9 Other Objects

Especially in wealthier burials an array of other objects appears. Literary texts are found sporadically in Theban tombs but are also attested at other places, such as Rifeh (Petrie 1907, 27). Bad organic preservation conditions at many sites make it hard to know how common these texts were. At Thebes there were also found several wooden boards with literary texts. Ostraca with literary texts are attested too. In the tomb of Sennedjem (TT1) at Thebes, dating under Sety I (1290–1279 BC) or Ramses II (1279–1213 BC) was found an unusually large ostracon with the Story of Sinuhe (Saleh, Sourouzian 1987, no. 220, 106 cm width, 22 cm height). Writing equipment can appear in burials too (Pinarello 2015, 52–85).

Game boards and gaming pieces should also be noted. They appear sporadically and are known from several places, such as Qau (Quirke 2005) and Zawiyet el Aryan, near Saqqara (Dunham 1978, 73). The senet game board (with a set of game pieces for a board with three by ten fields) is most common and certainly also had a religious function for the afterlife (Crist, Dunn-Vaturi and Voogt 2016, 54–9). Musical instruments appear frequently too. These include flutes, lyres and lutes (Emerit, Elwart 2017). In some cases this led researchers to assume that these were burials of musicians (Smith 1992, 209).

Flowers were also placed in burials. Perhaps the most striking find is the assemblage of floral remains found in the burial of Sennefer at Deir el-Medina (Thebes), dating to the end of the 18th Dynasty. His burial chamber contained an impressive quantity of leafy branches and garlands and his mummy was adorned with further flower arrangements (Bruyère 1929, 52–3, pls. II, VI, X.4). There, they are perhaps best classified as personal, festive adornments. Sennefer is the most remarkable example of a burial with flowers (Bruyère 1937, 201). Further examples were found within other burial chambers too (Bruyère 1937, 201).

Clothing and linen are also attested in some Theban burials of the 18th Dynasty, but it seems that this was not seen as essential for equipping the dead (Smith 1992, 209–10).

4.10 Food

There is not yet any study looking systematically at food offerings in New Kingdom burials, and so this summary can give just a general outline. Food offerings are well attested in burials of all social levels (Smith 1992, 210–13). In burials closely connected to the royal court, even wrapped pieces of meat in special containers were found (Lakomy 2016, 198–202). At Sawama, pottery vessels often contained food, a grain mash in certain vessels was often found in bowls, while berries, ox bones and pomegranates also appear (Bourriau, Millard 1971 35). At Fadrus, animal bones and remains in vessels attest to food offerings (Säve-Söderbergh, Troy 1991, 179–81). At Sedment with its good organic preservation, food offerings are also well attested, including bread. Bread and fruits were sometimes found in baskets (Franzmeier 2017b, 28, 84, 166, 275, 276, 294, 310,

333, 385, 684, 941, 943, 944, 1095, 1097, 1508, 1511). At Gurob, dom fruits are mentioned several times in the excavation report (Brunton, Engelbach 1927, see tomb register). Many vessels found in burials were most likely food containers, but it is not always clear whether all of them actually contained foodstuff. It is evident that food offerings became rarer in the late 18th Dynasty and in the Ramesside Period when 'daily life objects' disappeared too. However, they are still sporadically attested (Hulková 2013, 90).

    Due to the poor organic preservation conditions, food offerings are not well attested in burials of the Southern Levant, but more recent excavations with better recording indicate that they were not uncommon (Braunstein 2011, 17; compare van den Brink et al. 2017, 124–6).

5 Summaries

5.1 Summary: Time

There are many well-equipped burials in cemeteries dating to the early New Kingdom, in Egypt and Nubia, covering the period from around 1550 to 1400 BC. In contrast, there are very few cemeteries securely datable to the end of the Ramesside Period, around 1100 BC. For Nubia, it has even been claimed that the province was depopulated (Adams 1984, 63; compare Williams 1992, 5). Smith concluded that local wealth decreased over time, and related this to the impact of imperialism (Smith 2020, 382–3).

    The early 18th Dynasty is perhaps the period when Egyptian burials for a wider spectrum of the population were most richly equipped with household goods and personal adornments. In this period, burials were mostly equipped with objects of daily life, sometimes including used furniture. Pottery vessels are most common and are best preserved in the archaeological record. Cosmetic objects, including stone vessels and personal adornments, appear often too. The development reached a peak perhaps shortly before Hatshepsut (1479–1458 BC) and Thutmose III (1470–1425 BC), while under the following reigns the number of objects in burials was reduced.

    Evidently burial customs changed over time. Especially in the Ramesside Period, people were mainly buried with objects made for the afterlife, while daily life objects were in contrast rare. Burials of the very wealthiest people most likely were still filled with an array of objects, such as sarcophagi, canopic jars, shabti, amulets and perhaps further more ritual-related objects, such as the Book of the Dead. However, people who were not able to afford them did not find it necessary to place other objects into burials. The situation is entirely different to the change in mortuary customs in other periods of Egyptian history. In the Middle Kingdom, burials of the wealthier people were also full of objects just made for the burial, such as decorated coffins and wooden models showing servants and craftsmen at work. Funerary jewellery was also an important component of these burials (Grajetzki 2014b). Burials of the working population are less well documented for the period, but the few examples show that these people were equipped with at least some pottery vessels, and women with some personal adornments. No such practice is visible in the Ramesside Period. The wealthiest had elaborate sets of coffins, but those with few resources were buried in almost empty graves.

A decline in the number of burial goods is already visible within the 18th Dynasty. At Fadrus, in Nubia, the wealthiest burials belong to the early 18th Dynasty (Spence 2019, 557; Smith 2020, 382–3). The same observation can be made at Rifeh, even though the cemetery is only incompletely published. For the New Kingdom burials there, the focus of the excavation report is clearly on providing a pottery typology. Therefore, only the number of pottery types found in a burial is recorded. For the reconstruction of burial practices, this report can only be used as a rough guide. Nevertheless, the picture that emerges is clear. Before the reign of king Thutmose III (1470–1425 BC), burials were packed with pottery (Petrie 1907, pl. XXVIII m), then after this reign, pottery vessels became less common and disappeared almost completely with the Ramesside Period (Grajetzki 2020b, 104–5). It might be argued that the cemeteries at Rifeh decreased in importance over the course of the New Kingdom, however the numerous Ramesside shabtis found provide evidence for the continuing presence of burials in this period (Petrie 1907, pl. XXVIII c). They just no longer contained pottery to the same extent as before. A similar picture emerges from Sedment. From the early 18th Dynasty come several well-equipped burials, where daily life objects dominate the picture. The 19th Dynasty is also well attested at the site, but the burials are now dominated by objects made for the tomb, some of them of the highest quality, as several high court officials were buried here (Franzmeier 2017a, 95). At Amarna there appears a comparable picture. Kemp noted previously that burial goods are not that common there (Kemp 2013, 262).

What was involved in this change? Are there similar developments in other periods of Egyptian history? In the Middle Kingdom, a comparable pattern can be seen. There are many burials of less wealthy people dating up to the reign of the 12th Dynasty king Senusret I, whereas few are datable to the later part of the 12th Dynasty. It has been argued that this might relate to an impoverishment of the working population; their graves dropped out of the horizon of visibility in the archaeological record (Grajetzki 2020a, 155, 167–8). Is a similar scenario possible for the 18th Dynasty under the ruling queen Hatshesput (1479–1458 BC) and under Thutmose III (1470–1425 BC)? It is well established that the reign of Hatshepsut is a turning point in the New Kingdom (Galán 2014).

Many new developments are found in art and culture. It remains to be researched whether there were also new measures in controlling people. However, under the warrior king Thutmose III who was her successor, a militarisation of society is visible and one wonders whether many young men were drawn from the provinces to fight in the king's wars. Resources, including people, were taken away from the regions.

As mentioned before, for Fadrus and Nubia, Smith (2020, 382–3) observed a similar trend in burial patterns to that seen in Egypt. Smith interprets this as 'the ultimately negative impacts of the empire on the larger Nubian populace'. With all due reservation, it might be asked whether the same happened in Egypt proper.

So, it seems clear, from, the archaeological record that a polarisation of wealth is visible in the New Kingdom. The wealthier parts of society became richer, leaving the working population with fewer resources. This might be a result of some sort of 'inner colonisation' imposed internally on the Egyptian and Nubian population. Higher tax burdens, more corvée work for temple buildings and taking men out of communities for military enterprises might be the main contributing factors. This inner colonisation is a thorough exploitation of the working population within Egypt proper and in Nubia.

Social polarisation is often seen as one feature of state formation (Svizzero, Tisdell, 2014) but it is also often visible after the phase of the establishment of a state (compare for Athens: Blanton, Fargher 2008, 96). It therefore fits well into the image we have from the early New Kingdom, especially from the reigns of Hatshepsut (1479–1458 BC) and Thutmose III (1470–1425 BC). Egypt was now again able to mobilise all resources, including the people of the countryside.

A change in religious belief over what was important for placing into the tomb might be another reason for the disappearance of burial goods from graves of the working population. Peter Dorman (2014, 2–4) noticed many changes in funerary culture, especially under the Hatshepsut, and sees a 'reconceptualization of preparations for the afterlife'. He refers to the growing importance of mummiform coffins, but also to standardisation of the Book of the Dead. The transformation of the deceased into a new being equipped for the new life in the Underworld and ready for the journey into the Underworld became prominent. Here, evidently, a shift in focus is visible. Certain types of burial goods were no longer essential. This is perhaps most clearly visible in the pottery. In the early New Kingdom, food containers and tableware dominated the picture in the archaeological record of burials, whereas after Thutmose III, cosmetic containers are more common (Bourriau 1981, 72). In the Ramesside Period these types are often replaced by vessels used in embalming rituals or as shabti containers. The nourishment of the dead person was evidently no longer an essential part of the burial equipment.

The reduction in burial goods reached its peak in the Ramesside Period and is visible in all areas of mortuary culture and at all social levels (Fig. 15). Tomb chapels concentrate in their decoration on the world of deities, rituals and the Underworld (Assmann 1987, 37; Kampp-Seyfried 2003). The deceased is often shown offering and adoring different deities. Daily life scenes became rare. The tombs of the wealthiest officials are impressive monuments, but those who could not afford this did not consider it important to place other objects into a burial. In the late Ramesside Period, around 1100 BC, even monumental tombs of the wealthiest became less common, perhaps a reflection of the unstable economic conditions of the period (Jansen-Winkeln 2002, Cooney 2011).

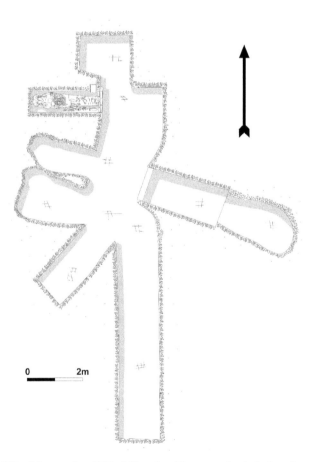

Figure 15 Burial complex 705 at Gurob with one unlooted chamber, redrawn from tomb card. The chamber contained the burial of a woman with coffin, shabti, a shabti box and a basket (drawing: author).

5.2 Summary: Class

In the future a comprehensive new dataset with statistics on tomb size and the value of burial equipment would substantially advances our understanding of the social profile of cemeteries. In the meantime, the general introduction can draw on a range of excavation reports, as well as more recent studies on the subject (Wada 2007, compare Smith 1992, 217–22; Lemos 2017, 124).

The cemetery of Fadrus in Lower Nubia has often been a focus of discussion on social profile (Grajetzki 2003, 73–6, Spence 2019, 547–9; Smith 2020, 381–3). The tombs in the region around Fadrus (Fig. 16) include all social levels and range from interments without any grave goods at all to those with decorated

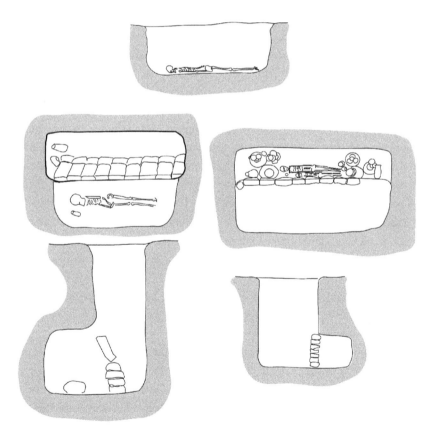

Figure 16 Three burials found at Fadrus, a simple, not very deep shaft tomb with few objects, a shaft tomb with small chamber and a few objects and a shaft tomb with chamber, two burials and a high number of burial goods. (Säve-Söderbergh, Troy 1991) (drawing: author)

tomb chapels. The latter belong to a local ruling class with links to the central government. In the final publication of the main burial ground at Fadrus proper, the social profile of the burials was evaluated (Säve-Söderbergh /Troy 1991: 224–5). All together, about 690 tombs were found, excavated, recorded and fully published. Five social ranks were distinguished. Social rank 1 are the tombs without finds, amounting to about 23 per cent of the burials. Social rank 2 were graves with one to four pottery vessels making up about half of the burials found. About 20 per cent of burials belong to social rank 3 with more than four pots. These three social ranks already make up 90 per cent of all burials. These are the poorest-equipped graves. Burials of social rank 4 contain pottery vessels, but also metal objects, such as metal vessels or weapons. The burials of social rank 5 contained all these goods, but also mummy masks. The burial chamber was paved with mud-bricks. The tombs with decorated tomb chapels that belong to the local ruling class were not included in the initial social ranking of the Fadrus cemetery as they are not part of the cemetery proper but belong to the same region. They could be classified as social rank 6, belonging to the wealthiest and most powerful people.

Coffins were a common feature of all burials, expect for the lowest social group. Only the burials of the two highest social levels had objects specifically produced for the burial, such as mummy masks. They also contained luxury items, such as metal objects. These two highest social levels make up less than 10 per cent of the entire population buried here mainly in the Eighteenth Dynasty. The rest of the population was evidently poorer but still had access to a range of items. Only about 23 per cent of the burials were found without any grave goods, but the conditions for the preservation of organic materials were not very good at Fadrus and possibly matting or objects such as baskets or clothing were included, but had decayed without leaving a trace. The ethnic background and occupation of the people buried here at Fadrus is not known, but the site certainly represents a rural community far from the centres of power at Thebes and Memphis. It is impossible to connect these people with specific professions. Do the poorer burials belong to farmers and the richer ones to landowners? We cannot tell from this archaeological record. The excavators wondered whether the wealth visible in the cemetery reflects the status of the related settlement as a market town (Säve-Söderbergh,Troy 1991, 249).

Looking at Egypt, the evidence from Amarna points to a very high number of people with few resources. Most people buried here would be in Fadrus social rank 1 or 2, very few in higher ones. Here two factors might be important. Perhaps a high number of workers were housed at Amarna without family members and social roots in the region (Stevens 2017, 119). Furthermore, burial customs, as discussed above had already changed, a point already indicated by Kemp when he summarised the evidence for the burial goods (Kemp 2013, 262).

Even without evaluating the social profile from tomb size statistics or from counting the number of burial goods at Amarna, the general picture seems clear. There is a high number of poorly equipped burials, and few with funerary objects (stelae and decorated coffins). There are some shaft tombs perhaps belonging to better off craftsmen and artists (Stevens 2017, 105) and there are the highest state officials with their decorated rock-cut tombs, placed in the mountains near the ancient city. The resources that those people had for a burial were extraordinarily high in comparison to the bulk of the population.

The burials at Amarna invite comparison with the excavated houses that Christian Tietze (1985) evaluated. He found three social groups in the houses. The ruling class comprised the highest officials of the king. About 7– 9 per cent of the houses, the biggest and best equipped, belong to them. Then there is a middle level of people, defined by Tietze as middle-ranking officials and leading craftsmen with medium-sized houses, that represent about 34– 37 per cent of the houses. Finally, the bulk of the population lived in the smallest and least well built houses. They represent about 54–59 per cent of the population. Interestingly, these three strata do not translate easily into the pattern of the cemeteries, where the simple surface burials are by far the most numerous, and so it must be assumed that many of those people from the middle-sized houses were buried in simple surface burials. The surface burials sometimes contained decorated coffins and stelae, so they did not automatically belong to people with few resources. On the other side there are the largest houses with up to fifty examples, far more than the number of large, decorated rock-cut tombs at Amarna. Therefore not all those officials in the largest houses had a large decorated rock-cut tomb at the site; some might have been buried somewhere else, others perhaps in shaft tombs.

5.3 Summary: Region

Egypt

Within Egypt, local variations in burial customs are visible, although the uneven archaeological records make it hard to pinpoint these differences. Especially in the 18th Dynasty there is an evident division between Thebes and the rest of the country. Thebes was the religious centre and capital of the country. The wealthiest burials there contained a high number of objects made for the graves. Decorated, mummiform coffins, shabtis and canopic jars appear here regularly, but are rare at other places even for graves of the well-to-do. At the end of the

18th Dynasty and in the Ramesside Period, the picture changed slightly. Memphis had been an important burial ground for the highest state officials already under Hatshepsut (1479–1458 BC), but now many of these objects made for the burial also appear in the provinces. A particularly notable change is the spread of mummiform coffins all over the country.

Beside this contrast of capital(s) and province, certain further regional differences are visible. For example the pottery coffins of the Ramesside Period are more common in the northern parts of Egypt (Petrie 1907, 22) than in the south. In contrast to that, early 18th Dynasty plaster masks are more common in Upper Egypt (and in Nubia) and are not well attested in the north (Rogge 1988a). In other cases, the archaeological record is not conclusive. At the cemeteries at Rifeh in Upper Egypt were found many Ramesside shabtis, whereas in the cemeteries of Qau (Petrie 1907, 22, pl. XXVIIC), only a few of them were discovered (Brunton 1930, 17). The two sites are not far apart. Are these local differences, or is that just an accident of the surviving record? Did the excavators just not uncover the tombs of that period at Qau that belong to the social level of people who could afford shabtis (Brunton 1930, 13)?

Nubia

While there is no single monograph yet on New Kingdom Nubian burial customs, there are some summaries within encyclopaedias (Spence 2019) and general discussions in books on Nubia and other topics (Smith 2003, 136–66, Lemos 2020, Smith 2020, 381–2).

Several times Nubian burials have been used as examples, as burial customs are similar to those in Egypt proper. Places such as Saï, Fadrus and Qustul are well excavated and well published, indeed to a higher standard than many contemporary Egyptian cemeteries. As a result, ironically, it is sometimes easier to assess Egyptian burial customs from sites in Nubia than from the Egyptian heartland.

At the beginning of the New Kingdom, several cemeteries belonging to the Nubian C-Group and Kerma culture were still used in Lower Nubia (Williams 1992, 2–3; Spence 2019, 541), but they seem to disappear early on and gave way to burial grounds following mainly Egyptian-style practice. Going further south, there are Nubian-style burials still attested within the New Kingdom. Several were, for example, recorded at Tombos near the Third Cataract (Smith 2003, 157–66). In contrast, already before the New Kingdom, many Egyptians lived in Lower Nubia and were buried according to Egyptian burial tradition.

There is a considerable discussion about the extent to which these burials were Egyptian or whether they relate rather to Nubian traditions (Säve-Söderbergh, Troy 1991, 7–13; van Pelt 2013, 539; Török 2009, 276–9; Smith 2015; Spence 2019, 561–2; Smith 2020, 381–2). Some have argued that burial customs were only superficially Egyptian (Török 2009, 278–9; van Pelt 2013, 539; Lemos 2020). The evidence so far presented in this book shows that the burials are fully within Egyptian tradition. The tombs at Saï provide many objects best known from ruling-class burials at Thebes or Saqqara. There is hardly another provincial cemetery within Egypt proper with such a high percentage of objects especially made for the burial, such as shabtis, heart scarabs or decorated and mummiform coffins. The tomb chapels were decorated with paintings. The common use of black coffins seems to particularly indicate a strong link to Theban burial tradition. This link is also visible in the use of funerary cones at Tombos (Smith 2003, 140–3).

At several places in Lower Nubia, rock-cut tombs decorated in Egyptian style were found (Hoffmann 1935; Fitzenreiter 2004). At Debeira there were also a number of well-preserved coffins which follow Egyptian designs, but the decoration appears crude (Taylor 2017). This is in contrast to many coffin remains found at other Nubian sites that are well made (Williams 1992, 153–8, pls. 30–2). One wonders whether the latter are products of Theban workshops, while those found at Debeira are rougher local copies.

At Fadrus, objects especially made for the burial are much rarer and those tombs appear then in their equipment much closer to the ones found at many provincial Egyptian sites. However, there is no ready way to evaluate the afterlife beliefs of those people buried at Fadrus and Saï. Their ethnicity also remains largely unknown.

Lower Nubia seems to have been flooded with Egyptian daily life objects. The pottery is almost identical to that found in Upper Egypt, although often locally made (Helmbold-Doyé, Seiler, 2019, 3, 36). This obviously does not tell us much about the ethnicity of these people. Indeed, even if there were burials with several Nubian-made local objects, that does not mean that these people were Nubians. These could be Egyptians just using local products in their household and in their burials. Nevertheless, for Lower Nubia, it is known that already in the late Middle Kingdom many Egyptians moved there to work in the fortresses. Inscriptions at Buhen provide names and titles of these people (Smith 2003, 78–83).

From all the evidence available so far, burial customs in Lower Nubia are similar or identical to those in Egypt proper. There might be some local variations, but regional diversity is also visible within Egypt. This is to be expected in a large empire (Svyantek, Mahoney 2002).

The late 18th Dynasty trend placing fewer objects into burials is also found in Lower Nubia. The development reaches its climax in both regions in the Ramesside Period, to an extent that some researchers proposed that Nubia was depopulated (p. 49). Instead the shared Nubian and Egyptian patterns might lead us to believe that religious ideas in both regions were closely related if not identical.

Southern Levant

As in the case with Nubia, there is a considerable discussion about the ethnicity of the people buried in the Southern Levant (Killebrew 2005, Gzella 2014). Unlike Nubia, there are also a number of monographs on burial customs in the region (Stiebing 1970, Gonen 1992).

The Southern Levant is not a homogenous region with a single uniform culture. At the coast in the early Iron Age (ca. 1200 – 1100 BC) people appear that are called in later sources the Philistines. In the central, mountainous region of the later kingdom of Israel other cultural traditions flourished.

When comparing Nubia, Egypt and the Southern Levant, a different picture emerges for the latter. In archaeology there is a stark decline around 1600 BC in the numbers of settlements visible, shortly before the Egyptians arrived. The reasons for and the exact nature of this is disputed but has been related to changes in society in general meaning many smaller sites were abandoned, while life in bigger towns went on (Greenberg 2019, 282, 285–7). At the beginning of the 18th Dynasty the region then came under Egyptian control and remained under Egyptian domination up to the end of the Ramesside Period. The exact nature of this rule is disputed, but it seems that the degree of control was rather loose in the 18th Dynasty. There were several city states that had to pay tributes periodically (Braunstein 2011, 1). Only in the Ramesside Period is there good archaeological evidence for some sort of direct Egyptian presence, with Egyptian officials active and living at several places. Egyptian-style buildings, perhaps residences of governors, were built, mainly in the regions closest to Egypt (Greenberg 2019, 300).

Burials customs in the Levant have many points in common with those in Egypt, but there are also significant differences. Natural rock caves of suitable shape and size were often selected and arranged as places for burials. Here sometimes bodies and grave goods were placed over several generations. However, single entombments are well attested too, in the same manner as in Egypt and Nubia. In terms of burial goods, a similar range of objects as in Egypt are attested in the Late Bronze Age and the Iron Age. There are many pottery vessels, personal adornments and weapons. Burials were flooded with Egyptian objects (Greenberg 2019, 304–5), though not to the same extent as in Nubia. In the Iron Age they made up about one third of items in the mortuary context (Mumford 2006, 166–7, 194, fig. 23-11). Egyptian personal adornments dominate some burials. The latter include many Egyptian-style scarabs, making many of these burials superficially Egyptian looking. About fifty pottery coffins were found at Deir el-Balaḥ (close to Sinai) and

Figure 17 Face of pottery coffin found at Tell Fara (from Petrie 1930, pl. XXIV)

several more at other places (Figs 17–18). They were often found in graves with many further items.

However, there are also discrepancies in relation to Egyptian mortuary practices. Perhaps the most important difference is the treatment of the body. In Egypt there is a certain care for the body. Coffins are common at least for people with some small wealth. Those who could not afford coffins were wrapped in mats or into some cloth. Hardly anything like this is attested in the Southern Levant. Coffins are rare even at places with better organic preservation. In both regions, multiple burials appear. In Egypt, when a new dead body arrived in a burial chamber, the old ones were left in place, whereas in the Southern Levant bones were pushed aside without much concern about their order (Braunstein 2011, 22–3). A further striking difference is the high number of lamps found in the burials in the Southern Levant while they are rare in Egyptian burials. They seem to indicate a markedly different concept of the afterlife.

Braunstein (2011) has investigated these burial goods in detail. Placing many items into burials was not a custom in Ramesside Egypt, but was still a custom in the Southern Levant. It seems evident that religious beliefs were different here and not influenced by Egyptian customs, unlike Lower Nubia where

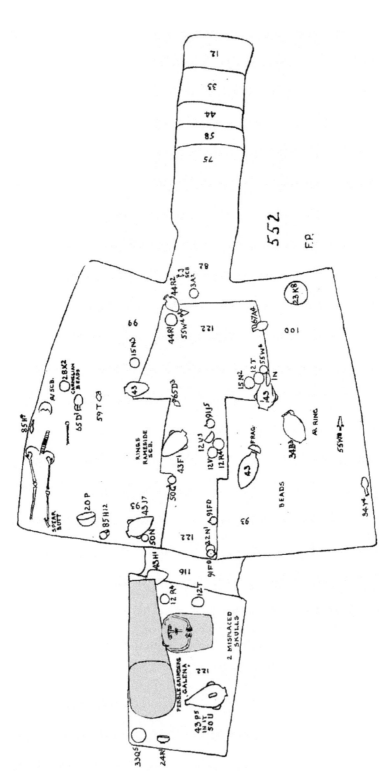

Figure 18 Example of a burial at Tell Fara with clay coffin (marked grey, in chamber on left) (Petrie 1930, pl. XIX)

Ramesside burials of less wealthy people were almost empty of goods, just as in Egypt proper.

The situation seems rather different in the towns where Egyptians lived. Egyptian stelae with short accurate texts and Egyptian-style relief depictions were found at Deir el-Balaḥ. The stelae come from illicit excavations but belong most likely to the cemeteries where anthropoid coffins were also excavated (Ventura 1987). Greenberg (2019, 299) summarised that 'Its material culture . . . point to a considerable indigenous population serving a thin stratum of officials who presented themselves as Egyptian.'

6 Concluding Remarks

The synopsis of New Kingdom burial customs reveal from the start the shortcomings in Egyptian archaeology. The focus in research is all too often on monuments and monumental art. Sites with spectacular finds are over-represented. The burials of the working population are not often the target of excavations. They are still badly known. The situation is better in Nubia, where the archaeological research seems to be more balanced and covers whole regions systematically due to the first Aswan and the High Dam rescue projects.

Within the Egyptian New Kingdom, burial customs changed considerably. At the beginning of the period around 1550 BC to about 1450 BC, burials even of not so well-to-do people were filled with objects, mainly coming from daily life, but also used at funeral rituals. Under the ruling queen Hatshepsut (1479–1458 BC) the world of the dead changed. Daily life objects disappear from graves over the following generations. Objects especially made for the tombs become more common. Previously they had been restricted to the wealthiest and were typical for the cemeteries at the royal residence. For this change in mortuary practices, two factors can be taken into account. First, the belief world changed. The transformation of the deceased into a new 'life' form in the Underworld was seen as most important. For this, objects of daily life were no longer essential in burials. The eternal nourishment was still seen as neces-sary, as funerary texts reveal, but it was no longer regarded as important to guarantee it by placing storage vessels into the burials. The second factor is economic: from the reign of Hatshepsut, the 'inner colonisation' of the country might have impacted the burials of the working population. Those people became poorer and no longer equipped burials with objects now more needed by the living. In the Amarna period the new burial customs were already fully established. Burials there are in general not well equipped, although a few funerary stelae and decorated coffins were found at Amarna, showing that at least some people had more resources.

This image of burial customs in the late 18th Dynasty is, in the view in modern times, somehow distorted as those tombs of the wealthiest people are more opulently equipped than ever before and after. These include the well-preserved tomb of Tuya and Yuya (KV46), parents of queen Tiy, the tomb of Meryt and the architect Kha (TT8), and finally the burial of king Tutankhamun (KV62). These burials abound in all types of objects, but they belong to people either at or closely connected to the royal court. The poorly equipped burials at Amarna belong to the other end of the social pyramid, providing evidence for the stark social division in the late 18th Dynasty.

In the Ramesside Period, all social levels, including the ruling classes, placed mainly objects made for the burials into tombs, especially shabtis and many amulets, which are now typical items in better-off graves all around the country. Daily life objects, even personal adornments, are rare. The same pattern of burial goods is also clearly visible in Nubia. There is much discussion about the ethnicity of the people there, but the general trend in burial customs is very close to that observed in Egypt proper. The picture is very different in the Southern Levant, although in the Ramesside Period even Egyptian-style pottery coffins were used as a container of the deceased. Burials are full of Egyptian-style objects, many of them produced in Egypt. Yet, in contrast to Egypt and Nubia, the big shift from daily life to funerary objects in burials is not visible in the Southern Levant. Egypt's imperialism did not have a deeper impact on the religious habitus there.

Abbreviations

BMPES	British Museum Publications on Egypt and Sudan
CRIPEL	Cahier de Recherches de l'Institut de Papyrologie et d'Égyptologie de Lille
FIFAO	Fouilles de l'Institut français d'archéologie orientale
GHP	Golden House Publications
IFAO	Institut Français d'Archéologie Orientale
JARCE	Journal of the American Research Center in Egypt
JEA	Journal of Egyptian Archaeology
KV + number:	tomb in the Valley of the Kings
MDAIK	Mitteilungen des Deutschen Archäologischen Instituts, Abteilung Kairo
SAAC	Studies in Ancient Art and Civilization
SAGA	Studien zur Archäologie und Geschichte Altägyptens
SAK	Studien zur Altägyptischen Kultur
TT + number:	Theban Tomb
ZÄS	Zeitschrift für ägyptische Sprache und Altertumskunde

Appendix: Examples of Burials and Cemeteries

(in each region in geographical order from north to south)

A.1 Egypt

A.1.1 Two burials at Saqqara

A typical burial of the 18th Dynasty was excavated in the surface layers above the Old Kingdom mastaba of Kagemni at Saqqara. Two bodies of women were found wrapped in linen within one coffin. The heads were oriented to the west. The burial goods were placed outside the coffin at the head end. These were mainly cosmetic objects, such as a comb, a cosmetic box and a cosmetic stone vessel with a small stick for eye paint. One box contained dom nuts and pomegranates. Several pottery jars were found too (Firth, Gunn, 1926, 69–70).

Another burial at Saqqara (Fig. A1) was found within a rectangular wooden coffin that according to the excavation report was covered with pitch. Inside was a skeleton lying on its back. Near the head was a small bottle and a bronze dagger, on the right was a wooden bow and there were three reed arrows. The burial goods are exceptional. Weapons appear in tombs, but they are not very common; metal weapons are evidently a prime target for looters, but we would expect some more to be preserved by chance. This burial raises many questions about the identity of the man buried here, although the weapons provide the strong impression of being related to the profession of this man. Inscriptional evidence is missing to confirm his name and profession (Firth, Gunn, 1926, 68). At least for the Old and Middle Kingdom there is a general consensuses that burials did not contain objects related to the profession of the tomb owners (Seidlmayer 2007). Did this custom change in the New Kingdom? The evidence presented in other burials speaks against that (Vogt 2013). Tools are not common; the bulk of the population were most likely farmers and we would expect some farming equipment in burials, but this is not the case. Perhaps objects related to a profession were only selected for burial where it had a certain status (Smith 1992, 209). This would fit the burial of a warrior in this instance at Saqqara. A further problem complicating the situation is the status of craftsmen. It is possible that many of the workmen had a serf-like status. That would suggest that they did not own the means of the production. Tools would have been owned by the institutions to which they were attached (Grajetzki 2020a, 134–5) and would therefore not appear in burials.

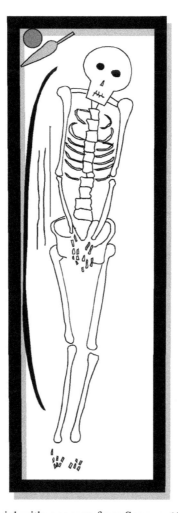

Figure A1 Burial with weapons from Saqqara (drawing: author)

A.1.2 Four burials at Gurob (Fig. A2)

Four relatively well-recorded graves found at Gurob may be discussed together. A drawing on the Gurob tomb cards provides some visual information rarely available for graves of the working population of the New Kingdom. Grave 218 was a simple surface burial in loose sand. There were no remains of a coffin, but patches of cloth might indicate that the woman here was wrapped in linen. Two vessels, a bowl and a vase were found at the head. One wonders whether the bowl was a symbolic food container, and the vase, a container for a drink. Grave 219 is more elaborate. The burial of this woman was placed within a very small mud-brick chamber with a flat roof. There were again remains of cloth, likely

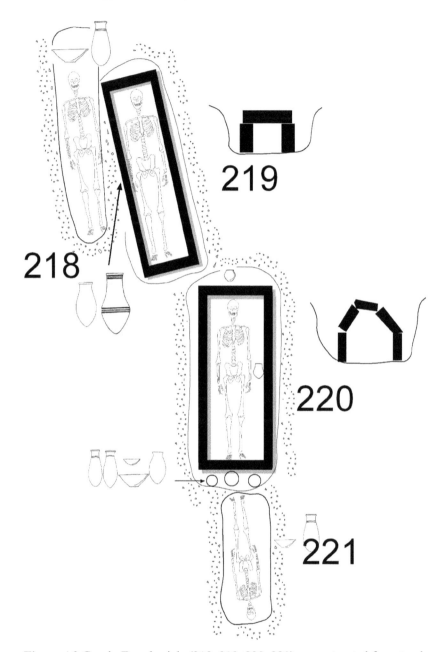

Figure A2 Gurob, Four burials (218, 219, 220, 221) reconstructed from tomb card (drawing: author)

again wrappings of linen for the body. Two bottle-like vessels were found on the right side. The tomb card and the publication do not say whether they were found in or next to the brick chamber. The vessels were perhaps containers for drinks. Grave 220 was the most elaborate of the four. It was again the burial of a woman, placed into a small burial chamber, that was slightly larger than those of grave 219. The roof consisted of a simple vault. The buried woman here is described on the tomb card as 'very old'. There were again remains of cloth. Five pottery vessels were found at the foot end, outside the brick chamber, three tall slim bottle-like vessels and two bowls. They might again be drink and food containers. One small vessel was found at the head end, outside the chamber, another small vessel inside the chamber. Grave 221 was a further simple surface burial of a woman, again with remains of cloth and two pottery vessels, one bowl and one bottle-like vessel. Unlike the other burials, her head was oriented to the south (Brunton, Engelbach 1927, pl. XV). The burials presented date most likely to the early 18th Dynasty (compare Wada 2007, fig. 7 on p. 364 for grave 220). These graves leave much space for speculation. The very old woman in grave 220 had the biggest grave with the highest number of pots. Had she reached some higher social status due to her old age, being the mother of several children that were able to provide burial goods? It is also remarkable that no personal adornments were found. They were evidently not seen as important for everyone, although younger women regularly received at least some.

A.1.3 Burial 431 at Gurob

Grave 431 at Gurob belongs most likely to the Ramesside Period (Brunton, Engelbach 1927, pl. XVII; Wada 2007, fig. 7 on p. 364). It was a burial of a child about 130 cm deep in the ground. There were remains of cloth and matting. Two medium-sized vessels were found at the head end. One is slightly funnel necked and is typical of the Ramesside Period. Comparable examples might have been used in rituals (Helmbold-Doyé, Seiler 2019, 225).

A.1.4 Qau 7360

An undisturbed burial (7360) at Qau was placed in a First Intermediate Period shaft tomb (Brunton 1930, 15, pl. XXIII). At the bottom of the shaft there was a chamber with the entrance still bricked up. The burial belonged to a man in a rectangular coffin; his face was covered with a gilded mummy mask. He was placed lying on his back with the head to the north. Tweezers and a stone vessel were found. Four beaker-like vessels were on the right side of the coffin. They are typical for the early New Kingdom and were most likely drinking vessels (compare p. 40). A bigger storage jar was found in the shaft in front of the blocked burial chamber. The man buried here evidently had some resources. The pottery equipment is not especially rich, but the gilded mask implies that some more resources were available to those who buried him.

A.1.5 Cemetery: Sawama

The cemetery of Sawama lies a few kilometres north of Akhmim and was excavated in 1914 (Bourriau, Millard 1971). One hundred and sixty-one tombs were uncovered, though for a few of them no information is available. The tomb architecture was most often rather simple. Most of the burials were shafts about 2 m deep, 2.2 m long and about 1 m wide. Twenty-two graves were about 3 m deep, only one was 14 m deep (tomb no. S. 105) and had two chambers at the bottom. There were remains of thirty-four wooden coffins, mostly undecorated wooden rectangular boxes, and a few plaster masks were found. The most common burial goods were pottery vessels, discovered in about seventy tombs. Stone vessels were found in thirty-six burials. Beads appear in forty-four burials, of which thirteen also had scarabs. Other personal adornments, such as earrings, are attested sporadically. Most of these objects are taken from daily life.

A burial that deserves special attention is S.66 B. It was found in a shaft, about 2.70 m deep and contained the remains of a woman placed in a rectangular coffin with the head to the south. There were traces of mummy wrappings. Near the head two pottery vessels were found, near the pelvis two stone cosmetic vessels, a basket and a mirror. A string of white beads, thirteen scarabs and pendants, two with the (king's) name Amenhotep, perhaps Amenhotep I (1514–1494 BC), were found around her pelvis. The burial seems to be simple. It remains unknown whether it was looted. However, the mirror is a metal object that might be expected to catch the attention of any robbers. This find indicates that the burial might be intact. Evidently, though the social status of this woman remains unknown, she had some resources.

A.1.6 Elaborate burial at Abydos, tomb E 294

This grave might serve as an example for the burial of members of a local ruling class in the early to mid 18th Dynasty 18th Dynasty (Fig. A3). A shaft tomb with chamber and two burials was found at Abydos in a rectangular sarcophagus that was sunk into the floor of the chamber. The seven-metre deep shaft that led to the chamber was partly bricked up. The main burial goods in the sarcophagus consisted of at least thirteen pottery and two stone vessels. They all seem to date to the early 18th Dynasty. The burial included a spindle-shaped jar with one handle, an import from the Levant contemporary with the early 18th Dynasty (for the date Wodzińska 2010, 190). There was also a bronze razor and a wooden kohl tube. Both bodies were covered with undecorated plaster. One body also had a mummy mask (Garstang 1900, 13, 26–7, pls. XVIII, XX). This burial belonged to people with

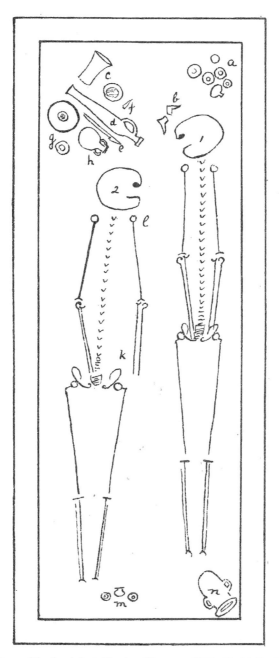

Figure A3 A wealthy burial at Abydos (Garstang 1900, 13, 26–7, pls. XVIII, XX)

substantial resources. Two bodies, side by side, indicate a couple. The sarcophagus in particular seems exceptional for this period; one wonders whether a Middle Kingdom example was reused.

A.2 Nubia

A.2.1 Tomb R 32 at Qustul

One simple burial of a mature woman was found at Qustul, perhaps dating to the mid-18th Dynasty. She was placed on the left side with the head to the north. The burial consisted of a shaft and a small chamber, the latter just big enough for the body and some burial goods. The chamber was blocked with bricks. Burial goods were found at the head and the feet. They included several pottery vessels and a kohl pot. The woman was adorned with several personal adornments; beads and earrings were found as well as several scarabs (Williams 1992, 17, 182–4 (tomb R 32)).

A.2.2 Burial 185/201 at Fadrus

The burial was at the bottom of a rectangular shaft. The deceased was placed into a mummiform coffin and mud bricks over the coffin formed some kind of roof or covering. Only one pottery vessel was found, at the head end. The burial is dated by the excavators to the period of Amenhotep II (1425–1400 BC) to Thutmose IV (1400–1390 BC) (Säve-Söderbergh, Troy 1991, 264, pl. 74). The equipment is simple but the mummiform coffin provides the impression that the person buried here had some resources, although burial goods appear not to have been considered important.

A.2.3 Grave S 588 at Semna

One example of a community burial place is tomb S 588 at Semna. It was a small chamber entered by a roughly cut staircase and filled with about sixteen bodies, probably all once placed in different wooden coffins. Burial goods within the chamber amounted to just four pottery vessels and several personal adornments, mostly beads of different materials, but also two ivory rings and amulets, including a Bes figure, two Taweret figures and a sun (?) disc between two horns (Dunham, Janssen 1960, 74, 101–2).

A.2.4 Burials at Saï

On the island of Saï there are the remains of a New Kingdom town with cemeteries. Parts of the cemeteries have been excavated and published to a high standard. Most burials so far uncovered seem to belong to the local ruling class. These are shafts with chambers and mud-brick chapels above ground. The chapels consisted of a courtyard and a pyramid behind. In a few cases there was an additional room in front of the pyramid. Remains of wall paintings were found in the chapels. There are also fragments of stelae. In the courtyard before the chapel there was most often a shaft leading down to several underground burial chambers with several interments. The burials were mostly found looted. Some other burials were just placed in single shafts. Several burials in one chamber were not uncommon. The burial goods contained a high number of objects of a funerary industry, including many examples of inscribed shabtis, amulets, inscribed heart scarabs and anthropoid coffins. The equipment gives a purely Egyptian impression. Daily life objects are rare; they include a mirror, and several stone vessels, most likely part of cosmetic equipment. One headrest was found too. Tomb 20 was best preserved (Minault-Gout, Thill 2012, 97–106). It dates to the Ramesside Period with some burials perhaps dating after the New Kingdom (Minault-Gout, Thill 2012, 411). The burial complex has three underground chambers. The smaller chamber (Cb) contained three bodies and the remains of a wooden anthropoid coffin and several shabtis, inscribed but not naming an owner. It seems that this chamber and the more heavily looted other small chamber were reserved for the highest status people buried here. In the main, bigger chamber were found fourteen skeletons placed here over a longer period of time and perhaps not all belonging to people of the same high social level.

A.3 Levant

A.3.1 Burial at Shadud

One burial that looks very Egyptian was found at Shadud. The deceased, perhaps a man, was placed in a pottery coffin that has a human face. Crossed hands are depicted directly under it. Ears and hair are only very schematically indicated. The man was richly adorned and had a dagger on the right side and a scarab on a gold ring on the left. The scarab bears the throne name of the Egyptian king Sety I (1290–1279 BC). Inside the coffin were also found small pottery vessels as well as a bronze bowl. Further burial goods were placed on the outside. The skull of a bovid was found at the head. Further bones were found scattered around, some in bowls, perhaps used for a funeral meal (van den Brink 2016; van den Brink et al. 2017).

A.3.2 Burial at Gezer

A relatively well-preserved cave tomb with burials dating from the mid-18th Dynasty to the end of the same dynasty was found at Gezer. The cave was originally used as cistern but was later converted into a burial place. It is a roughly round chamber, less than 4 m in diameter. The floor was covered with stone to provide an even surface. Some eighty individuals were placed there over a period of about one hundred years. It is unclear how the bodies were placed there, but it seems they were most often just roughly deposited along with some burial goods, pushing older burials aside. The special find is a Minoan clay coffin with two primary and ten further individuals. Clay coffins are not well attested in the Southern Levant before 1500 BC (Seger 1988, 114–15). This particular example might indicate that Minoans were living and were buried here. The finds in the tomb include a high number of foreign objects. There was a high percentage of Cypriote pottery, as well as a range of Egyptian objects such as a glass vessel, scarabs, an alabaster vessel and an ivory comb (Seger 1988, 50–1).

A.3.3 Tomb 114 at Deir el Balaḥ

The burial contained a pottery coffin with three or even four skeletons. Within the human-shaped coffin there were found several bronze knives and bronze vessels, most of them with parallels in Egypt and the Levant. In the coffin there was also found a golden amulet perhaps showing the Egyptian god Bes. Outside the coffin were found several pottery jars; there was a Mycenaean piriform jar, a Canaanite storage vessel and an Egyptian storage vessel. Several Egyptian style stone vessels were discovered too. Personal adornments found include a necklace of carnelian and gold beads, earrings and scarabs. One scarab bears the throne name of Ramses II (1279–1213 BC) and provides a terminus post quem for the burial (Dothan 1978, 5–27). The burial goods are partly Egyptian. A similar burial in the 18th Dynasty in Egypt proper would be no surprise, as even Mycenaean or Canaanite pottery can appear there too. However, placing several bodies in a coffin was not common in the 19th Dynasty and the high number of daily life objects is also no longer typical for this period.

A.3.4 Cemeteries of Tell Beit Mirsim

Many burials of the late Bronze Age and early Iron Age were excavated at Tell Beit Mirsim. They were discovered at salvage excavations, so the recording of finds is not always of the highest standard, but they still offer a rough picture. Burials were most often placed into natural caves around the small town. They were enlarged for the burials but only in the Iron Age II period (after 1000 BC) were there well-carved underground chambers (Ben-Arieh 2004, 3). Tomb 500 has a roughly square chamber, about 5 x 5.5 m wide and just about 1 m high. One hundred and fifty pottery vessels were found, other finds include a bronze needle, a bronze arrowhead, personal adornments and a stone game board. The pottery includes thirty-one lamps and Cypriot pottery. The burial was most likely in use over a longer period (Ben-Arieh 2004, 6, 21–4).

Glossary

ankh-sign an amulet, ankh is the symbol of life

button seal seal in the shape of a button, decorated on the underside with figures or floral motifs, often in a rather rough style

Canaan the ancient name of the Southern Levant

Cataract shallow parts of the Nile River, between Khartoum and Aswan, where the current is broken by numerous boulders and rocky outcrops

canopic jar/box container for the entrails of the deceased after mumification. Recently it had been argued that these jars were often not used for the entrails but instead were part of burial rites performed before the body of the deceased and the burial goods were placed into a burial chamber (Jirásková 2015).

djed pillar an amulet, symbolising stability

funerary cones pottery cones with inscriptions that decorated a tomb chapel, they are best attested at Thebes

heart scarab a scarab with a spell that commands the heart not to give evidence against the deceased, when he or she is being judged by Osiris, ruler of the Underworld. After mummification the heart was left in the body. The heart scarab was placed on the body beside the heart.

kohl substance used as eye paint, the main ingredient is galena or lead ore

mastaba part of the tomb structure at ground level over Old and Middle Kingdom burial chambers. Sometimes they are solid blocks with just a small chapel in front, but others contain many, sometimes decorated, rooms for the cult of the deceased.

Minoan the Bronze Age culture on Crete

mummy mask a mask placed over the head of a mummified body

Mycenaean the Bronze Age culture in Greece

natron a mixture of sodium carbonate and sodium bicarbonate, often used in mummification

pilgrim flask round bottle, common in Egypt from the New Kingdom onward

sarcophagus coffin in stone

shabti small mummiform figures, some of them are inscribed with a text that helped the deceased to avoid corvée work (unpaid labour)

soul house a house model made in clay, placed on burials of less wealthy people, mainly in the Middle Kingdom

stela an inscribed or decorated stone, often used as tomb stone but also found in separate offering chapels and structures

Story of Sinuhe a literary composition from the Egyptian Middle Kingdom, composed around 1900 BC and known from multiple copies in the following centuries

throne name the principal name an ancient king took upon acceding to the throne

tiyet pillars an amulet

vizier the highest Egyptian state official after the king

References

Adams, William Y. (1984). 'The First Colonial Empire: Egypt in Nubia, 3200–1200 BC', *Comparative Studies in Society and History* 26(1): 36–71.

Aldred, Cyril. (1971). *Jewels of the Pharaohs: Egyptian Jewellery of the Dynastic Period*. Thames and Hudson: London.

Andrews, Carol. (1994). *Amulets of Ancient Egypt*. British Museum Press: London.

Arnold, Dieter. (1976). *Gräber des Alten und Mittlerewn Reiches in El-Tarif*. von Zabern: Mainz.

— (2002). *The Pyramid Complex of Senwosret III at Dahshur Architectural Studies*. The Metropolitan Museum of Art: New York.

Assmann, Jan. (1987). 'Priorität und Interesse: Das Problem der Ramessidischen Beamtengräber', in Jan Assmann, Günter Burkard and Vivian Davies (eds.), *Problems and Priorities in Egyptian Archaeology*. KPI: London and New York, 31–41.

— (2001). *Death and Salvation in Ancient Egypt*. Cornell University Press: Ithaca and London.

Auenmüller, Johannes Stefan G. (2014). 'The Location of New Kingdom Elite Tombs: Space, Place and Significance', in Joanna Debowska-Ludwin, Mariusz A. Jucha and Piotr Kołodziejczyk (eds.), *Proceedings of the Sixth Central European Conference of Egyptologists. Egypt 2012: Perspectives of Research, SAAC 18, 2014, Studies in Art and Civilization* 18: 171–93.

Baines, John. (2006). 'Display of Magic in Old Kingdom Egypt', in Kasia Szpakowska (ed.), *Through a Glass Darkly: Magic, Dreams and Prophecy in Ancient Egypt*. Classical Press of Wales: Swansea, 1–32.

— (2009). 'Modelling the Integration of Elite and other Social Groups in Old Kingdom Egypt', in Juan Carlos Moreno García (ed.), *Élites et pouvoir en Égypte ancienne, CRIPEL* 29: 117–44.

Baines, John and Peter Lacovara. (2002). 'Burial and the Dead in Ancient Egyptian Society', *Journal of Social Archaeology* 2(1): 5–36.

Ben-Arieh, Sarah. (2004). *Bronze and Iron Age Tombs at Tell Beit Mirsim*. Israel Antiquities Authority: Jerusalem.

Blanton, Richard and Lane Fargher. (2008). *Collective Action in the Formation of Pre-Modern States*. Springer: New York.

Böhme, Isa. (2019). 'Botschafter der kosmischen Ordnung Thot, Geb, Horus und Dunanui und Tb 161 auf den privaten Sarkophagen des Neuen Reiches', in Marc Brose et al. (eds), *En détail: Philologie und*

Archäologie im Diskurs Festschrift für Hans-W. Fischer-Elfert, ZÄS Supplement 7, de Gruyter: Berlin, 103–31.

Borchardt, Ludwig. (1909). *Das Grabdenkmal des Königs Nefer-ir-ke-re.* Hinrichs: Leipzig.

Bosmajian, Haig A. (1969). 'The Language of White Racism', *College English* 31(3): 263–72.

Bourriau, Janine. (1981). *Pottery from the Nile Valley before the Arab Conquest.* Cambridge University Press: Cambridge.

Bourriau, Janine and Anne Millard. (1971). 'The Excavation of Sawâma in 1914 by G. A. Wainwright and T. Whittemore', *JEA* 57: 28–57.

Braunstein, Susan L. (2011). 'The Meaning of Egyptian-Style Objects in the Late Bronze Cemeteries of Tell el-Farʿah (South)', *Bulletin of the American Schools of Oriental Research*, 364: 1–36.

Brunton, Guy. (1930). *Qau and Badari III.* Bernard Quaritch: London.
    (1948). *Matmar.* Bernard Quaritch: London.

Brunton, Guy and Reginald Engelbach. (1927). *Gurob.* Bernard Quaritch: London.

Bruyère, Bernard. (1929). *Rapport sur les fouilles de Deir El Médineh (1928).* Institut français d'archéologie orientale: Cairo.
    (1937). *Rapport sur les fouilles de Deir el Médineh: 1933–1934. La Nécropole de l'Ouest.* Institut français d'archéologie orientale: Cairo.

Budka, Julia. (2017). 'Pyramid Cemetery SAC5, Sai Island, Northern Sudan: An Update Based on Fieldwork from 2015–2017', *Ägypten und Levante* 27: 107–30.

Casino, Emanuele. (2017). 'Remarks on Ancient Egyptian Cartonnage Mummy Masks from the Late Old Kingdom to the End of the New Kingdom', in Julia M. Chyla, Joanna Dębowska-Ludwin, Karolina Rosińska-Balik and Carl Walsh (eds.), *Current Research in Egyptology 2016, Proceedings of the Seventeenth Annual Symposium.* Oxbow Books: Oxford and Philadelphia, 56–73.

Cooney, Kathlyn M. (2011). 'Changing Burial Practices at the End of the New Kingdom: Defensive Adaptations in Tomb Commissions, Coffin Commissions, Coffin Decoration, and Mummification', *JARCE* 47: 3–44.

Cotelle-Michel, Laurence. (2004). *Les sarcophages en terre cuite en Egypte et en Nubie, de l'époque prédynastique à l'époque romaine.* Faton: Dijon.

Crist, Walter, Anne-Elizabeth Dunn-Vaturi and Alex de Voogt. (2016). *Ancient Egyptians at Play: Board Games across Borders.* Bloomsbury Academic: London.

Czerny, Ernst. (1999). *Tell el-Dab'a IX, Eine Plansiedlung des frühen Mittleren Reiches.* Austrian Academy of Sciences: Vienna.

Darnell, John Coleman and Colleen Manassa. (2007). *Tutankhamun's Armies, Battle and Conquest during Ancient Egypt's Late Eighteenth Dynasty*. John Wiley: Hoboken, New Jersey.

D'Auria, Sue (1988). 'Female Figure on a Bed', in Sue D'Auria, Peter Lacovara and Catherine H. Roehrig (eds.), *Mummies and Magic: The Funerary Arts of Ancient Egypt*. Museum of Fine Arts: Boston, 137, no. 74.

Davies, W. Vivian. (2013). 'The Tomb of Sataimau at Hagr Edfu: An Overview', *British Museum Studies in Ancient Egypt and Sudan* 20: 47–80.

Dorman, Peter F. (2014). 'Innovation at the Dawn of the New Kingdom', in José Galán, Betsy M. Bryan and Peter F. Dorman (eds.), *Creativity and Innovation in the Reign of Hatshepsut*. Oriental Institute Museum Publications 69, The Oriental Institute: Chicago, 1–6.

(2017). 'The Origins and Early Development of the Book of the Dead', in Foy Scalf (ed.), *Book of the Dead: Becoming God in Ancient Egypt*. Oriental Institute Museum Publications 39, The Oriental Institute: Chicago, 29–40.

Dothan, Trude. (1978). 'Excavations at the Cemetery of Deir el-Balah', *Qedem* 10: 1–114.

Driaux, Delphine. (2019). 'Toward a Study of the Poor and Poverty in Ancient Egypt: Preliminary Thoughts', *Cambridge Archaeological Journal* 30(1): 1–19.

Dunham, Dows and Jozef M. Janssen. (1960). *Second Cataract Forts I. Semna, Kumma*. Museum of Fine Arts: Boston.

(1978). *Zawiyet el Aryan: The Cemeteries Adjacent to the Layer Pyramid*. Museum of Fine Arts: Boston.

Eliezer D. Oren. (1973). *The Northern Cemetery of Beth Shan*. Brill: Leiden.

Emerit, Sibylle and Dorothée Elwart (2017). 'La musique à Deir el-Medina: vestiges d'instruments et iconographie du temple ptolémaïque d'Hathor', in Hanane Gaber, Laurie Bazin Rizzo and Frédéric Servajean (eds.), *À l'Œuvre on Connaît l'Artisan ... de Pharaon!* Silvana Editoriale: Milan, 131–7.

Emery, Walter B. (1961). *Archaic Egypt*. Harmondsworth and Baltimore: Penguin.

Engelbach, Reginald. (1915). *Riqqeh and Memphis IV*, School of Archaeology in Egypt. Bernard Quaritch: London.

(1923). *Harageh*. Bernard Quaritch: London.

Firth, Cecil, M. and Battiscombe Gunn. (1926). *Teti Pyramid Cemeteries I: Text*. L'institute François d'archéologie Orientale: Cairo.

Fitzenreiter, Martin. (2004). 'Identität als Bekenntnis und Anspruch: Notizen zum Grab des Pennut (Teil IV)', *Der Antike Sudan MittSAG15*: 169–93.

Frankfort, Henri J. D. and John D. S. Pendlebury. (1933). *The City of Akhenaten, Part II, The North Suburb and the Desert Altars: The Excavations at Tell el Amarna, during the Seasons 1926–1932*. Egypt Exploration Society, Oxford University Press: London.

Franzmeier, Henning. (2014). 'News from Parahotep: the small finds from his tomb at Sedment rediscovered', *JEA* 100: 151–79.

(2017a). *Die Gräberfelder von Sedment im Neuen Reich*, I. Brill: Leiden and Boston.

(2017b). *Die Gräberfelder von Sedment im Neuen Reich*, II. Brill: Leiden and Boston.

Friedman, Renée. (2007). 'The Nubian Cemetery at Hierakonpolis, Egypt: Results of the 2007 Season', *Sudan & Nubia* 11: 57–62.

Galal, Ahmed and David Aston. (2003). 'New Kingdom Anthropoid Pottery Coffins from Kom Abu Rady and Sedment', *Jaarbericht van het voora-ziatisch-egyptsich genootschap e Oriente Lux* 37 (2001–2002): 127–80.

Galán, José M. (2014). 'Preface', in José M. Galán, Betsy M. Bryan and Peter F. Dorman (eds.), *Creativity and Innovation in the Reign of Hatshepsut*. Studies in Oriental Civilization 69, The Oriental Institute of the University of Chicago: Chicago, Illinois, vii–xii.

Gander, Manuela. (2009). 'Materialimitationen Bemalte Gefäße aus Gräbern des Neuen Reiches aus dem Ägyptischen Museum und Papyrusssammlung Berlin', *Studien zur Altägyptischen Kultur* 38: 83–99, plates 2–5.

(2012). 'Imitation of Materials in Ancient Egypt', in Katalin Anna Kóthay (ed.), *Art and Society: Ancient and Modern Contexts of Egyptian Art, Proceedings of the International Conference held at the Museum of Fine Arts, Budapest, 13–15 May 2010*, Museum of Fine Arts: Budapest 265–71.

Garstang, John. (1900). *El Arábah: A Cemetery of the Middle Kingdom; Survey of the Old Kingdom Temenos; Graffiti from the Temple of Sety*. Bernard Quaritch: London.

(1907). *The Burial Customs of Ancient Egypt, as Illustrated by Tombs of the Middle Kingdom*. Archibald Constable: London.

Gatto, Maria Carmela. (2021). 'The A-Group and 4th Millennium BCE Nubia', in Geoff Emberling and Bruce Beyer Williams (eds.), *The Oxford Handbook of Ancient Nubia*. Oxford University Press: New York, 125–42.

Gonen. Rivka. (1992). *Burial Patterns and Cultural Diversity in Late Bronze Age Canaan*. Eisenbrauns: Winoan Lake, Indiana.

Graefe, Erhart. (2007). *Die Doppelgrabanlage "M" aus dem Mittleren Reich unter TT 196 im Tal el-Asasif in Theben-West*. Aegyptiaca Monasteriensia 5. Shaker: Aachen.

Grajetzki, Wolfram. (2003). *Burial Customs in Ancient Egypt*. Duckworth: London.

—— (2007). 'Multiple Burials in Ancient Egypt to the End of the Middle Kingdom', in Silke Grallert and Wolfram Grajetzki (eds.), *Life and Afterlife in Ancient Egypt during the Middle Kingdom and Second Intermediate Period*. Golden House Publications: London, 16–34.

—— (2010). *The Coffin of Zemathor and Other Rectangular Coffins of the Late Middle Kingdom and Second Intermediate Period*. Golden House Publications: London.

—— (2014a). 'The Tomb of Khnumhotep at Rifeh', in Aidan Dodson, John Johnston and Wendy Monkhouse (eds.), *A Good Scribe and Exceedingly Wise Man: Studies in Honour of W. J. Tait*. Golden House Publications: London, 100–11.

—— (2014b). *Tomb Treasures of the Late Middle Kingdom: The Archaeology of Female Burials*. University of Pennsylvania Press: Philadelphia.

—— (2016). 'An Early New Kingdom Coffin from Abydos', *Égypte Nilotique et Méditerranéenne* 9, 47–63 (www.enim-egyptologie.fr/index.php?page=enim-9&n=5 retrieved 08/02/2020).

—— (2020a). *The People of the Cobra Province in Egypt: A Local History, 4500 to 1500 BC*. Oxbow: Oxford and Philadelphia.

—— (2020b). 'Die Friedhöfe des Neuen Reiches bei Rifeh', *Sokar* 39: 98–105.

Greenberg, Raphael. (2019). *The Archaeology of the Bronze Age Levant*. Cambridge University Press: Cambridge and New York.

Guy, Philip L. O. (1938). *Megiddo Tombs*. The University of Chicago Oriental Institute Publications XXXIII. The University of Chicago Press: Chicago, Illinois.

Gzella, Holger. (2014). 'Peoples and Languages of the Levant During the Bronze and Iron Ages', in Ann E. Killebrew and Margreet Steiner (eds.), *The Oxford Handbook of the Archaeology of the Levant: c. 8000–332 BCE*. Oxford University Press: Oxford, 24–34.

Hafsaas, Henriette. (2021). 'The C-Group People in Lower Nubia: Cattle Pastoralists on the Frontier between Egypt and Kush', in Geoff Emberling and Bruce Beyer Williams (eds.), *The Oxford Handbook of Ancient Nubia*. Oxford University Press: Oxford, 159–77.

Helmbold-Doyé, Jana and Anne Seiler. (2019). *Die Keramik aus dem Friedhof S/SA von Aniba (Unternubien)*. De Gruyter: Berlin and Boston.

Hermann, Alfred. (1935). 'Das Grab eines Nakhtmin in Unternubien', *MDAIK* 6: 1–40.

Hornung, Erik, Rolf Krauss and David A. Warburton. (2006). *Ancient Egyptian Chronology*, Handbook of Oriental Studies I (83). Brill: Leiden and Boston.

Hulková, Lucia. (2013). 'Ein ramessidischer Friedhof zwischen Tell el-Dab'a und ^cEzbet Helmi'. Vienna. online thesis of the University Vienna http://othes.univie.ac.at/25386/ (retrieved 23/ 04/2017).

Ikram, Salima and Aidan Dodson. (1998). *The Mummy in Ancient Egypt, Equipping the Dead for Eternity*. Thames and Hudson: London.

Janák, Jiří. (2013). 'Akh', in Jacco Dieleman and Willeke Wendrich (eds.), *UCLA Encyclopedia of Egyptology*, Los Angeles. http://digital2.library.ucla.edu/viewItem.do?ark=21198/zz002gc1 pn (retrieved 15/06/21).

Jansen-Winkeln, Karl. (2002). 'Ägyptische Geschichte im Zeitalter der Wanderungen von Seevölkern und Libyen', in Eva Andrea Braun-Holzinger and Hartmut Mathäus (eds.), *Die nahöstlichen Kulturen und Griechenland an der Wende vom 2. zum 1. Jahrtausend. Kontinuität und Wandel von Strukturen und Mechanismen kultureller Interaktion*. Bibliopolis: Paderborn, 123–42.

Janssen, Jac. J. (1975). 'Economic History during the New Kingdom', *SAK 3*, 127–85.

Jéquier, Gustave. (1933). *Deux pyramides du Moyen Empire*. L'Institut Français d'archéologie Orientale: Cairo.

(1940). *Le Monument Funéraire de Pepi II. Tome III, Les Approches du Temple*. L'Institut Français, d'archéologie Orientale: Cairo.

Jirásková, Lucie. (2015). 'Damage and Repairs of the Old Kingdom Canopic Jars: The Case at Abusir', *Prague Egyptological Studies*: 76–85.

Kampp-Seyfried, Friederike. (2003). 'The Theban Necropolis: An Overview of Topography and Tomb Development from the Middle Kingdom to the Ramesside Period', in Nigel Strudwick and John H. Taylor (eds.), *The Theban Necropolis: Past, Present and Future*. The British Museum Press: London, 2–10.

Kenyon, Kathleen M. (1960). *Excavations at Jericho – Volume I, Tombs Excavated in 1952–4*. School of Archaeology in Jerusalem: London.

Kemp, Barry. (2013). *The City of Akhenaten and Nefertiti, Amarna and its People*. Thames and Hudson: London.

Killebrew, Ann E. (2005). *Biblical Peoples and Ethnicity: An Archaeological Study of Egyptians, Canaanites, Philistines, and Early Israel, 1300–1100 BCE*. Society of Biblical Literature Archaeology and Biblical Studies 9, Society of Biblical Literature: Atlanta, Georgia.

Lakomy, Konstantin C. (2016). *Der Löwe auf dem Schlachtfeld, Das Grab KV 36 und die Bestattung des Mairherperi im Tal der Könige*. Reichert: Wiesbaden.

Lemos, Rennan. (2017). 'Material Culture and Social Interactions in New Kingdom Non-Elite Cemeteries', in Julia M. Chyla, Joanna Dębowska-Ludwin, Karolina Rosińska-Balik and Carl Walsh (eds.), *Current Research in Egyptology 2016 Proceedings of the Seventeenth Annual Symposium Jagiellonian University, Krakow, Poland 4–7 May 2016*, Oxbow Books: Oxford and Philadelphia.

    (2020). 'Material Culture and Colonization in Ancient Nubia: Evidence from the New Kingdom Cemeteries', in Claire Smith (ed.), *Encyclopaedia of Global Archaeology*. Springer: New York.

Lilyquist, Christine. (2003). *The Tomb of Three Foreign Wives of Thutmosis III*. Yale University Press: New Haven and London.

Loat, Leonard. (1905). 'Gurob', together with Margaret Murray. *Saqqara Mastabas*, part I–II. British School of Archaeology in Egypt and B. Quaritch: London.

Maspero, Gaston. (1895). *Manual of Egyptian Archaeology and Guide to the Study of Antiquities in Egypt*, trans. Amelia B. Edwards. H. Grevel: London.

Milde, Henk. (2012). 'Shabtis', in Willeke Wendrich (ed.), *UCLA Encyclopedia of Egyptology*, Los Angeles. http://digital2.library.ucla.edu/viewItem.do?ark=21198/zz002bwv0z (retrived 17/06/2021).

Minault-Gout, Anne and Thill, Florence. (2012). *Saï II, Les cimetière des tombes hypogées du Nouvel Empire*, Texte, Planches, FIFAO 69. Institut français d'archéologie orientale: Cairo.

Miniaci, Gianluca. (2011). *Rishi Coffins and the Funerary Culture of Second Intermediate Period Egypt*. GHP Egyptology 17. Golden House Publications: London.

    (2014). 'The Case of the Third Intermediate Period "Shabti-Maker (?) of the Amun Domain" Diamun/Padiamun and the Change in Conception of Shabti Statuettes', *JEA* 100: 245–73.

    (2019). 'Burial Demography in the Late Middle Kingdom: A Social Perspective'. in Rune Nyord (ed.), *Concepts in Middle Kingdom Funerary Culture: Proceedings of the Lady Wallis Budge Anniversary Symposium held at Christ's College, Cambridge, 22 January 2016*. Peeters: Leiden and Boston: 117–49.

Moskos, George. (1984). 'Marguerite Duras's "Moderato Cantabile"', *Contemporary Literature*, 25(1): 28–52.

Mumford, Gregory. (2006). 'Egypt's New Kingdom Levantine Empire and Serabit el-Khadim, Including a Newly Attested Votive Offering of Horemheb', *Journal of the Society for the Study of Egyptian Antiquities* 33: 159–203.

Munro, Irmtraut. (1988). *Untersuchungen zu den Totenbuch-Papyri der 18. Dynastie*. Keagan and Paul: London New York.

Münch, Hans-Hubertus. (2000). 'Categorizing Archaeological Finds: The Funerary Material of Queen Hetepheres I at Giza', *Antiquity* 74(286): 898–908.

Näser, Claudia. (2001). 'Zur Interpration funerärer Praktiken im Neuen Reich: Der Ostfriedhof von Deir el-Medine', in Caris-Beatrice Arnst, Ingelore Hafemann and Angelika Lohwasser (eds.), *Begegnungen, Antike Kulture im Niltal.* Helkmar Wodkte und Katharina Stegbauer: Leipzig, 373–98.

(2013). 'Equipping and Stripping the Dead', in Liv Nilsson Stutz and Sarah Tarlow (eds.), *The Oxford Handbook of the Archaeology of Death and Burial.* Oxford University Press: Oxford, 643–61.

(2017). 'Structures and Realities of the Egyptian Presence in Lower Nubia from the Middle Kingdom to the New Kingdom: the Egyptian cemetery S/SA at Aniba', in Neal Spencer, Anna Stevens and Michaela Binder (eds.), *Nubia in the New Kingdom: Lived Experience, Pharaonic Control and Indigenous Traditions. Proceedings of the July 2013 Conference at the British Museum.* BMPES 3. Peeters: Leuven, 557–74.

Niwiński, Andrzej. (1988). *21st Dynasty Coffins from Thebes, Chronological and Typological Studies.* Theben 5. von Zabern: Mainz.

(2014). 'Did the Pat-People and the Rekhyt-People have Different Burial Ceremonies?', in Mariusz A. Jucha, Joanna D, Bowska-Ludwin and Piotr Kołodziejczyk (eds.), *Aegyptus Imago Caelo. Studies presented to Krzysztof M. Ciałowicz on his 60th Birthday.* Jagiellonian University in Kraków: Kraków, 253–60.

Nyord, Rune. (2017). '"An Image of the Owner as He Was on Earth": Representation and Ontology in Middle Kingdom Funerary Images', in Gianluca Miniaci, Marilina Betrò and Stephen Quirke (eds.), *Company of Images: Modelling the Imaginary World of Middle Kingdom Egypt (2000–1500 BC).* Peeters: Leuven, Paris, Bristol, CT, 337–59.

(2018). '"Taking Ancient Egyptian Mortuary Religion Seriously": Why Would We, and How Could We?', *Journal of Ancient Egyptian Interconnections* 17 (March): 73–87.

Odler, Martin. (2015). 'Copper Model Tools in Old Kingdom Female Burials', in Massimiliano S. Pinarello, Justin Yoo, Jason Lundock and Carl Walsh (eds.), *Current Research in Egyptology 2014.* Oxbow: Oxford: 39–58.

Oren, Eliezer D. (1973). *The Northern Cemetery of Beth Shan.* Brill: Leiden

Otto, Eberhard. (1975). 'Ach', in Wolfgang Helck and Eberhard Otto (eds.), *Lexikon der Ägyptologie* I. Otto Harrassowitz: Wiesbaden, 49–51.

van Pelt, W. Paul. (2013). 'Revising Egypto-Nubian Relations in New Kingdom Lower Nubia: From Egyptianization to Cultural Entanglement', *Cambridge Archaeological Journal*, 23(3): 523–50.

Petrie, W. M. Flinders. (1890). *Kahun, Gurob, and Hawara*. Trench, Trübner: London.

(1891). *Illahun, Kahun and Gurob*. David Nutt: London.

(1907). *Gizeh and Rifeh*. British School of Archaeology in Egypt, Bernard Quaritch: London.

(1914). *Amulets*. Constable: London.

(1930). *Beth-Pelet I (Tell Fara)*. Publications of the Egyptian Research Account 48, Bernard Quaritch: London.

Petrie, William M. Flinders and Guy Brunton. (1924). *Sedment* II. British School of Archaeology in Egypt, Bernard Quaritch: London.

Petrie, Flinders W. M., G. A. Wainwright and E. Mackay. (1912). *The Labyrinth, Gerzeh and Mazghuneh*. British School of Archaeology in Egypt. Bernard Quaritch: London.

von Pilgrim, Cornelius. (2021). 'Middle Kingdom Settlement Geography at the First Cataract', in Alejandro Jiménez-Serrano and Antonio J. Morales (eds.), *Middle Kingdom Palaces Culture and Its Echoes in the Provinces*. Harvard Egyptological Studies 12, Brill: Leiden and Boston, 393–416.

Pinarello, Massimiliano Samuele. (2015). *An Archaeological Discussion of Writing Practice: Deconstruction of the Ancient Egyptian Scribe*. GHP Egyptology 23. Golden House Publications: London.

Pinch, Geraldine. (2003). 'Redefining Funerary Objects', in Zahi Hawass and Lyla Pinch Brock (eds.), *Egyptology at the Dawn of the Twenty-first Century: Proceedings of the Eighth International Congress of Egyptologists Cairo, 2000, 2 History Religion*. The American University in Cairo Press: Cairo and New York, 443–7.

Polz, Daniel. (1991). 'Die Särge aus Schacht 2 der Grabanlage', in Jan Assmann, *Das Grab des Amenemope (TT41)*. von Zabern: Mainz, 244–67.

(1995). 'Bericht über die 4. und 5. Grabungskampagne in der Nekropole von Dra' Abu el-Naga/Theben West', *MDAIK* 51: 207–25.

Poole, Frederico. (1999). 'Social Implications of the Shabti Customs in the New Kingdom', in Rosanna Pirelli (ed.), *Egyptological Studies for Claudio Barocas*. Istituto Universitario Orientale: Naples, 95–113.

Porten, Bezalel (ed.). (2011). *The Elephantine Papyri in English*. Documenta et Monumenta Orientis Antiqui, vol 22. Brill: Atlanta.

Pouls Wegner, Mary-Ann. (2015). 'Anthropoid Clay Coffins of the Late Bronze Age to Early Iron Age in Egypt and the Near East: A Re-

Evaluation of the Evidence from Tell El-Yahudiya', in Timothy P. Harrison, Edward B. Banning and Stanley Klassen (eds.), *Walls of the Prince: Egyptian Interactions with Southwest Asia in Antiquity*. Culture and History of the Ancient Near East, vol. 77. Brill: Leiden and Boston: 292–315.

Prell, Silvia. (2019). 'Burial Customs as Cultural Marker: A "Global" Approach', in Manfred Bietak and Silvia Prell (eds.), *The Enigma of the Hyksos, volume I: ASOR conference Boston 2017 – ICAANE conference Munich 2018 – Collected papers*. Harrassowitz: Wiesbaden, 124–47.

Quack, Joachim Friedrich. (2009). 'Grab und Grabausstattung im späten Ägypten', in Angelika Berlejung and Bernd Janowski (eds.), *Tod und Jenseits im alten Israel und in seiner Umwelt*, Forschungen zum Alten Testament 64. Mohr Siebeck: Tübingen, 597–62.

Quirke, Stephen. (2005). 'Gaming-Board Squares', in Betsy Teasley Trope, Stephen Quirke and Peter Lacocara (eds.), *Excavating Egypt*. Michael C. Carlos Museum, Atlanta, 126–7. no. 95.

(2013). *Going out in Daylight – prt m hrw: The Ancient Egyptian Book of the Dead – Translation, Sources, Meanings*. GHP Egyptology 20. Golden House Publications: London.

Randall-Maciver, David and Arthur C. Mace. (1902). *El Amrah and Abydos, 1899–1901*. Egypt Exploration Fund: London.

Randall-Maciver, David and Leonard C. Woolley. (1911). *Buhen* (2 volumes: Text, Plates). University Museum Philadelphia: Philadelphia.

Raven, Maarten J. (2005). 'Egyptian Concepts on the Orientation of the Human Body', *JEA* 91: 37–53.

Richards, Janet. (2005). *Society and Death in Ancient Egypt: Mortuary Landscape of the Middle Kingdom*. Cambridge University Press: Cambridge.

Rogge, Eva. (1988a). 'Face from a Mummy Mask', in Sue D'Auria, Peter Lacovara and Catherine H. Roehrig (eds.), *Mummies and Magic: The Funerary Arts of Ancient Egypt*. Museum of Fine Arts: Boston, 132, no. 65.

(1988b). 'Face from a Mummy Mask', in Sue D'Auria, Peter Lacovara and Catherine H. Roehrig (eds.), *Mummies and Magic: The Funerary Arts of Ancient Egypt*. Museum of Fine Arts: Boston, 132–3, no. 66.

Roth, Ann Macy. (1988). 'Tomb Group of a Woman', in Sue D'Auria, Peter Lacovara and Catherine H. Roehrig (eds.), *Mummies and Magic: The Funerary Arts of Ancient Egypt*. Museum of Fine Arts: Boston, 76–7, no. 6.

Saleh, Mohamed and Hourig Sourouzian. (1987). *Official Catalogue, The Egyptian Museum Cairo*. von Zabern: Mainz.

Sartini, Lisa. (2015). 'The Black Coffins with Yellow Decoration: A Typological and Chronological Study'. *Egitto e Vicino Oriente* 28: 49–66.

Säve-Söderbergh, Torgny and Lana Troy. (1991). *New Kingdom Pharaonic Sites: The Finds and the Sites*. The Scandinavian Joint Expedition to Sudanese Nubia vols 5:2 and 5: 3. Almqvist and Wiksell: Uppsala.

el-Sawi, Ahmed. (1979). *Excavations at Tell Basta, Report of Seasons 1967–1971 and Catalogue of Finds*. Charles University: Prague.

Schäfer, Heinrich. (1908). *Priestergräber und andere Grabfunde von Ende des Altens Reichs bis zur griechischen Zeit vom Totentempel des Ne-use-rê*. J. C. Hinrichs'sche Buchhandlung: Leipzig.

Schneider, Hans D. (2012). *The Tomb of Iniuia*. Brepols: Tunhout.

Seger, Joe D. (1988). *Gezer V: The Field I Caves*. Ben-Zvi Printing Enterprises: Jerusalem.

Seidlmayer, Stephan. (1990). *Gräberfelder aus dem Übergang vom Alten zum Mittleren Reich*. SAGA 1, Heidelberger Orientverlag: Heidelberg.

(2001). 'Die Ikonographie des Todes', in Harco Willems (ed.), *Social Aspects of Funerary Culture in the Egyptian Old and Middle Kingdoms: Proceedings of the International Symposium Held at Leiden University 6–7 June, 1996*. Peeters: Leuven, 205–52.

(2006). 'Der Beitrag der Gräberfelder zur Siedlungsarchäologie Ägyptens', in Ernst Czerny, Irmgard Hein, Hermann Hunger, Dagmar Melman and Angela Schwab (eds.), *Timelines: Studies in Honour of Manfred Bietak*, vol. I, Peeters: Leuven, Paris, Dudley, MA, 309–16.

(2007). 'People at Beni Hassan: Contributions to a Model of Ancient Egyptian Rural Society', in Zahi A. Hawass and Janet Richards (eds.), *The Archaeology and Art of Ancient Egypt: Essays in Honor of David B. O'Connor 2*. Supreme Council of Antiquities: Cairo, 351–68.

Serpico, Margaret. (2008). 'Sedment', in Jan Picton and Ivor Pridden (eds.), *Unseen Images, Archive Photographs in the Petrie Museum, Volume I: Gurob, Sedment and Tarkhan*. Golden House Publications: London, 99–180.

Smith, Mark. (2017). *Following Osiris: Perspectives on the Osirian Afterlife from Four Millennia*. Oxford University Press: Oxford.

Smith, Stuart Tyson. (1992). 'Intact Theban tombs of the Seventeenth and Eighteenth Dynasties from Thebes and the New Kingdom Burial System', *MDAIK* 48: 193–231.

(2003). *Wretched Kush: Ethnic Identities and Boundaries in Egypt's Nubian Empire*. Routledge: London and New York.

(2015). 'Hekanefer and the Lower Nubian Princes Entanglement, Double Identity or Topos and Mimesis', in Hans Amstutz, Andreas Dorn,

Mathias Müller, Miriam Ronsdorf and Sami Uljas (eds.), *Fuzzy Boundaries, Festschrift für Antonio Loprieno*, II. Widmaier: Hamburg: 767–79.

(2020). 'The Nubian Experience of Egyptian Domination During the New Kingdom', in Geoff Emberling and Bruce Beyer Williams (eds.), *The Oxford Handbook of Ancient Nubia, the New Kingdom*. New York: Oxford University Press, 369–94.

Spence, Kate. (2019). 'New Kingdom Tombs in Lower and Upper Nubia', in Dietrich Raue (ed.), *Handbook of Ancient Nubia*. De Gruyter: Berlin and Boston, 541–66.

Spencer, Neil. (2009). 'Cemeteries and a Late Ramesside Suburb at Amara West', *Sudan & Nubia* 13: 47–62.

Staring, Nico. (2015). 'Studies in the Saqqara New Kingdom Necropolis: From the Mid-19th Century Exploration of the Site to New Insights into the Life and Death of Memphite Officials, Their Tombs and the Use of Sacred Space' (unpublished PhD). Sydney, Australia.

Stevens, Anna. (2017). 'Death and the City: The Cemeteries of Amarna in their Urban Context'. *Cambridge Archaeological Journal* 28(1): 103–26.

(2018a). 'Beyond Iconography: The Amarna Coffins in Social Context', in John H. Taylor and Marie Vandenbeusch (eds.), *Ancient Egyptian Coffins, Craft Traditions and Functionality*, BMPES 4. Peeters: Leuven, Paris, Bristol, CT: 139–60.

(2020). 'Excavations the North Desert Cemetery', *JEA* 106(1–2): 3–7.

Stevens, Anna and Gretchen Dabbs. (2017). 'The North Tombs Cemetery Excavations and Skeletal Analysis', *JEA* 103: 137–49.

Svizzero, Serge and Clement Tisdell. (2014). 'Inequality and Wealth Creation in Ancient History: Malthus' Theory Reconsidered', *Economics and Sociology*, 7(3): 222–39.

Svyantek, Daniel J., Kevin T. Mahoney and Linda L Brown. (2002). 'Diversity And Effectiveness in the Roman and Persian Empires', *The International Journal Of Organizational Analysis*, 10(3): 260–83.

Stiebing, William Henry. (1970). *Burial Practices in Palestine during the Bronze Age*. University Microfilms: Ann Arbor, Michigan.

Taylor, John H. (2017). 'The Coffins from Debeira: Regional Interpretations of New Kingdom Funerary Iconography', in Neil Spencer, Anna Stevens and Michaela Binder (eds.), *Nubia in the New Kingdom: Lived Experience, Pharaonic Control and Indigenous Traditions*. Peeters: Leuven, 537–56.

Tietze, Christian (1985). 'Amarna: Analyse des Wohnhäuser und soziale Struktur der Stadtbewohner', *ZÄS* 112: 48–84.

Török, László. (2009). *Between Two Worlds: The Frontier Region between Ancient Nubia and Egypt, 3700 BC–AD 500*, Probleme der Ägyptologie 29. Brill: Leiden.

van den Brink, Edwin C. M. (2016). 'Clay Coffin with Anthropoid Lid', in Daphna Ben Tor (ed.), *Pharaohs in Canaan: The Untold Story.* The Israel Museum: Jerusalem, 128–30, no. 51.

van den Brink, Edwin C. M. and Ron Beeri et al. (2017). 'A Late Bronze Age II Clay Coffin from Tel Shaddud in the Central Jezreel Valley, Israel: Context and Historical Implications', *Levant* 49(2): 105–35.

van Driel-Murray, Carol. (2000). 'Leatherwork and Skin Products', in Paul T. Nicholson and Ian Shaw (eds.), *Ancient Egyptian Materials and Technology.* Cambridge University Press: Cambridge, 299–319.

Ventura, Raphael. (1987). 'Four Egyptian Funerary Stelae from Deir el-Balaḥ', *Israel Exploration Journal* 37(2/3): 105–15.

Vogt, Katharina. (2013). 'Berufsbezogene Beigaben oder Status- und Prestigeobjekte? Kontextanalyse spezifischer Grabbeigaben aus nicht-königlichen Bestattungen des Neuen Reiches'. in Neunert, Gregor, Kathrin Gabler, and Alexandra Verbovsek (eds.), *Nekropolen: Grab – Bild – Ritual. Beiträge des zweiten Münchner Arbeitskreises Junge Aegyptologie (MAJA 2), 2. bis 4. 12.2011.* Harrassowitz: Wiesbaden: 233–52.

Wada, Koichiro. (2007). 'Provincial Society and Cemetery Organization in the New Kingdom', *SAK* 36: 347–89.

Wodzińska, Anna. (2010). *A Manual of Egyptian Pottery, Volume 3: Second Intermediate Period–Late Period.* Ancient Research Associates: Boston.

Weill, Raymond. (1938). 'Ceux qui n'avaient pas de tombeau dans l'Égypte ancienne', *Revue del'histoire des religions*, 118: 5–32.

Willems, Harco. (2014). *Historical and Archaeological Aspects of Egyptian Funerary Culture.* Brill: Leiden and Boston.

Williams, Bruce Beyer. (1992). *New Kingdom Remains from Cemeteries R, V, S and W at Qustul and Cemetery K at Adindan.* The Oriental Institute Chicago: Chicago.

Zillhardt, Ruth. (2009). *Kinderbestattungen und die soziale Stellung des Kindes im alten Ägypten: Unter besonderer Berücksichtigung des Ostfriedhofes von Deir el-Medine.* Göttinger Miszellen, Beihefte 6. Seminar für Ägyptologie und Koptologie der Universität Göttingen: Göttingen.

Zivie, Alain. (2003). *Les tombeaux retrouvés de Saqqara.* du Rocher: Paris.

Acknowledgments

I am grateful to Gianluca Minicia, Juan Carlos Moreno García and Anna Stevens for accepting this text for Elements. Special thanks goes to Stephen Quirke for reading my English. Further thanks for discussions, pictures and literature goes to Claudia Näser, Lutz Franke, Jan Picton, Ivor Priten, Valentina Gasperini, Catriona Wilson and Stephanie Boonstra.

This book is dedicated to Hans Litten.

Cambridge Elements ☰

Ancient Egypt in Context

Gianluca Miniaci

University of Pisa

Gianluca Miniaci is Associate Professor in Egyptology at the University of Pisa, Honorary Researcher at the Institute of Archaeology, UCL – London, and Chercheur associé at the École Pratique des Hautes Études, Paris. He is currently co-director of the archaeological mission at Zawyet Sultan (Menya, Egypt). His main research interest focuses on the social history and the dynamics of material culture in the Middle Bronze Age Egypt and its interconnections between the Levant, Aegean, and Nubia.

Juan Carlos Moreno García

CNRS, Paris

Juan Carlos Moreno García (PhD in Egyptology, 1995) is a CNRS senior researcher at the University of Paris IV-Sorbonne, as well as lecturer on social and economic history of ancient Egypt at the École des Hautes Études en Sciences Sociales (EHESS) in Paris. He has published extensively on the administration, socio-economic history, and landscape organization of ancient Egypt, usually in a comparative perspective with other civilizations of the ancient world, and has organized several conferences on these topics.

Anna Stevens

University of Cambridge and Monash University

Anna Stevens is a research archaeologist with a particular interest in how material culture and urban space can shed light on the lives of the non-elite in ancient Egypt. She is Senior Research Associate at the McDonald Institute for Archaeological Research and Assistant Director of the Amarna Project (both University of Cambridge).

About the Series

The aim of this Elements series is to offer authoritative but accessible overviews of foundational and emerging topics in the study of ancient Egypt, along with comparative analyses, translated into a language comprehensible to non-specialists. Its authors will take a step back and connect ancient Egypt to the world around, bringing ancient Egypt to the attention of the broader humanities community and leading Egyptology in new directions.

Cambridge Elements ≡

Ancient Egypt in Context

Elements in the Series

Seeing Perfection: Ancient Egyptian Images Beyond Representation
Rune Nyord

Ethnic Identities in the Land of the Pharaohs: Past and Present Approaches in Egyptology
Uroš Matić

Egypt and the Desert
John Coleman Darnell

Coffin Commerce: How a Funerary Materiality Formed Ancient Egypt
Kathlyn M. Cooney

Ceramic Perspectives on Ancient Egyptian Society
Leslie Anne Warden

The Nile: Mobility and Management
Judith Bunbury and Reim Rowe

The Archaeology of Egyptian Non-Royal Burial Customs in New Kingdom Egypt and Its Empire
Wolfram Grajetzki

A full series listing is available at: www.cambridge.org/AECE

CPSIA information can be obtained
at www.ICGtesting.com
Printed in the USA
BVHW041739250122
627144BV00009B/57